MELISSA ALTMAN LINSKY

THE LITTLE BOOK

BOOK

of

BASKETBALL LAW

AMERICAN BAR ASSOCIATION
Defending Liberty
Pursuing Justice

Cover design by Andrew O. Alcala/ABA Publishing.

17 16 15 14   5 4 3

The Library of Congress Cataloging-in-Publication is on file.

ISBN: 978-1-61438-943-9

Discounts are available for books ordered in bulk. Special consideration is given to state bars, CLE programs, and other bar-related organizations. Inquire at Book Publishing, ABA Publishing, American Bar Association, 321 North Clark Street, Chicago, Illinois 60654-7598.

www.ShopABA.org

*This book is dedicated with love to
my Super Stars Tyler and Max.
Always dream big and
shoot for the stars!*

Table of Contents

Introduction

The idea for a "little book" on basketball law came about while I was reading *The Little White Book of Baseball Law* in preparation for the Sports Law class I teach each year. I was trying to find a source where students could learn about cases in an easy-to-relate-to manner that was both entertaining and informative. I found the baseball "little book" offered an enjoyable and refreshing take on baseball cases and encouraged my students to read it. Since my work experience is in hockey and basketball, while reading the baseball "little book," I kept thinking of all the equivalent cases that related to those sports and searched to see if a similar book existed on either topic. As one did not, I proposed to write them, beginning with basketball.

This book is written in line with how I speak—rather informally—and you can envision hand gestures accompanying the words "well" and "so." Each chapter title poses a question or premise, which the text then answers and discusses by telling the story of one or more cases. Most case information comes from the decision or decisions cited in the chapter title. Where information comes from other sources, such as the complaints, briefs, books, or related news articles, it is noted.

Some of the cases are ones you will repeatedly come across when reading casebooks, such as Kareem Abdul-Jabbar's trademark and right of publicity suit against General Motors, and movie producer Irving Levin's attempt to purchase the Celtics over the NBA's objections. They answer the questions: "What rights do basketball players have in their own names and images?" and "Can the NBA prevent the sale of one of its franchises?" The Abdul-Jabbar case is juxtaposed against a more recent case involving another former Laker, Shaquille O'Neal.

Other chapters focus on newer or quirky cases not found in casebooks, but which may influence the field nonetheless. For example, *George v. NCAA* focuses on the NCAA's ticket allocation system for its Men's Basketball Championship and whether it violated Indiana Lottery laws. *TIG Insurance Co. v. Workers' Compensation Appeals Board and David Feitl* highlights the issue of California's cumulative trauma statute that professional basketball teams face regularly. The statute, in general, allows for athletes to collect workers' compensation for life from a non-California-based team. Although some decisions are changing the way these cumulative trauma cases are handled and legislation is being proposed to curtail California's long-arm jurisdiction in this area, it is not a well-known aspect of sports law.

The "To the Hoop" sections either highlight an area of law discussed in the chapter, provide a hopefully interesting fact, give updates with current applications of the cases, or note some practice points.

As you read this book, please keep a few things in mind. First, although the book offers what I hope is an enlightening description of decisions, it should not be used as a substitute for legal advice. You should seek a lawyer for advice on your specific issue. Second, as in the other "little books" in the series, the cases used are simplified and focus on only those parts of each decision that answer the question or premise posed in the chapter title. They lack the details and other issues you will find from reading the full opinions. I encourage you to read the entire case for a complete picture.

I hope that the book provides you with insight into how different jurisdictions have handled things like ticket distribution, renewal rights to season tickets, an athlete's rights of publicity, the use of eminent domain for the building of a basketball arena, player-to-player injuries, franchise movement, sexual harassment, and more.

Some words of thanks . . .

I am filled with gratitude for my brother Joshua Altman. I could not have written this book without his assistance. He reviewed the proposal from the onset, helped with creating chapter titles and was my sounding board through the entire two-and-a-half-year process. He read every draft of every draft and provided me with critical feedback on organization and civil procedure. A lawyer in his own right, he could tell me whether my renditions of cases made sense to someone outside of the sports realm. I am forever grateful for his time and support.

I also want to thank dear friends and Emory Law graduates Jeannette Moore, Lynn Carrico, Ellyn Pearlstein, and Jamie Kitces for reviewing drafts of chapters and providing assistance related to their areas of expertise.

I would like to thank Scott Wilkinson for providing me with my foray into sports law. Without the opportunity and lessons he provided, I would never have entered this field. After Turner sold the Atlanta Hawks, Atlanta Thrashers, and operating rights to Philips Arena, Scott, as the new company's general counsel, took me under his wing. I could not have worked for or learned from a better example. He garners the respect of everyone he encounters with his unwavering honesty and integrity. In addition, he understood the dividing forces that working moms have for work and family and found a way for two moms to share job responsibilities. On that note, I would also like to acknowledge my former colleague and dear friend, Caren Cook. Sharing a position only works when you have someone that you wholeheartedly trust and respect.

And last, but definitely not least, I wish to thank my parents, Cheryl and Howard Altman, for their constant, unconditional encouragement and support during the writing process and always.

Happy reading!

THE LITTLE
BOOK
of
BASKETBALL LAW

ABA
AMERICAN BAR ASSOCIATION
Defending Liberty
Pursuing Justice

Chapter 1

Lightly Seasoned Tickets:
The Rights of Season Ticket Holders

In re William Harrell, 73 F.3d 218 (9th Cir. 1996);
In re Liebman, 208 B.R. 38 (Bankr. N.D. Ill. 1997);
Brotherson v. Prof. Basketball Club, L.L.C.,
604 F. Supp. 2d 1276 (W.D. Wash. 2009)

You have season tickets for your favorite basketball team and have renewed them for the past ten seasons on a yearly basis. Now there is a wait list for season tickets and you want to sell the ability to renew your tickets on the open market, hoping that anyone on that wait list would jump at the chance to buy those renewal rights. Can you cash in?

This issue of renewal rights came to light in bankruptcy proceedings. The debtors had season tickets for popular teams and the bankruptcy trustees attempted to sell the right to renew those season tickets to maximize the estate's revenue. The teams opposed that scheme.

Take the 1992 Phoenix Suns. At the start of the 1992 season, the Suns had four consecutive playoff berths and Charles Barkley had just joined the roster. By April 1993, the Suns were headed to the NBA Finals and had a 600- to 700-person wait list for season tickets, which increased to 1,200 names by January

1994. In addition, these fans paid the team $100 per seat just to be placed on a season ticket wait list.[1]

William and Carol Harrell, holders of four Suns season tickets for thirteen years, filed for bankruptcy in December 1992.[2] The bankruptcy trustee wanted the Harrells to turn over their season tickets and their renewal rights for future season tickets to the bankruptcy court for inclusion in the bankruptcy estate. The trustee wanted to sell the remainder of the 1992–93 regular season tickets, including the Harrells's ticket account for 1993 playoff tickets and their renewal rights for future season tickets.

The Suns[3] opposed the trustee's motions. The team argued that the estate should not include rights to renew tickets because only *property* belongs in the estate and there is no *property* right in renewing season tickets.

After various motions and filings, the question of whether the right to renew season tickets is a property right and subject to inclusion in the trustee's estate, came before the 9th Circuit.

The 9th Circuit noted that all of a debtor's property interest goes into the bankruptcy estate. However, because the bankruptcy code doesn't define what constitutes a property interest, the court needed to review Arizona law for its definition of property.

Under Arizona law, a mere expectation of renewal of an interest in property is not a property right. The court analogized the renewal rights in tickets to landlord-tenant law. In doing so,

---

1. Appellate Brief, 1994 WL 16059532 (C.A.9) at 4, United States Court of Appeals, 9th Circuit, *In re: William V. Harrell, et ux., Debtor, Robert P. Abele, Trustee, Appellant v. Phoenix Suns Limited Partnership, Appellee*, No. 94-16057, Aug. 18, 1994. Lower Court Docket Number: CV-93-00854-SMM, on appeal from the United States District Court for the District of Arizona.

2. Appellate Brief, 1994 WL 16059532 at 4.

3. The Harrells opposed the motion as well. But this chapter focuses on the Suns' arguments.

it found that the right to renew a lease is at the lessor's discretion, unless the lease expressly gives the tenant a right to renew.

Although season ticket holders are generally awarded the opportunity to renew their tickets, no language in the season ticket contract gives them that right; the Suns are not contractually obligated to renew a season ticket holder's account each year. The 9th Circuit, then, held that a season ticket holder's expectation of a renewal of season tickets is not a property right and does not belong in the bankruptcy estate.

A similar scenario occurred with the Chicago Bulls.

The Bulls won the NBA Finals three years in a row, in '91, '92, and '93, lost in the semifinals in '94 and '95, and won the Finals again in '96, '97, and '98. Upon Michael Jordan's return from retirement in 1995, Bulls season tickets were "greatly prized in the Chicagoland area."[4] This was the situation when Chicago Bulls season ticket holder Warren S. Liebman filed for bankruptcy.

The bankruptcy trustee wanted to sell Liebman's renewal rights in his Bulls season tickets, but the Bulls objected.

In ruling for the Bulls, the bankruptcy judge reviewed other cases, including the *Suns* decision discussed above. The judge also examined the season ticket holder agreement and past conduct between the parties to determine his answer.

The judge looked to the contract. The Bulls clearly stated their policy in all pertinent material: (1) The season ticket invoice states that "[s]eason tickets are offered on a one-year basis"; (2) the playoff ticket invoice says that "[e]ach season and playoff ticket is a revocable license"; and (3) letters sent to season ticket holders state that "[t]he Bulls reserve the right to review all accounts before offering season tickets for the [next] season."[5]

---

4. *In re Liebman*, 208 B.R. 38 (Bankr. N.D. Ill. 1997) at 39.
5. *In re Liebman* at 40.

Thus, a Bulls season ticket holder has nothing more than a license to purchase tickets, which the Bulls may revoke at any time.

In addition, the bankruptcy judge said that past conduct by the Bulls to renew tickets did not ripen into a property interest. The bankruptcy trustee placed significant weight on the Bulls' past practices of automatically renewing season tickets if the account was current and, generally, only revoking season tickets for misconduct. But, the judge said: "The expectation that the tickets would be renewed, however realistic, does not ripen into a property interest."[6]

However, the judge indicated that parties may agree otherwise, and *agree otherwise* is just what happened in Seattle.

In 2006, Howard Schultz, coffee entrepreneur extraordinaire, sold the Seattle SuperSonics to Clay Bennett, chairman and owner of Professional Basketball Club, LLC (PBC). The sale was steaming with controversy at the onset. The combination of reports that Schultz was growing disillusioned with owning a basketball team[7] and that Bennett hoped to bring a team to Oklahoma City[8] created the perfect brew for a move. Nonetheless, after purchasing the team, Bennett sought public financing to either restore Key Arena, where the Sonics played, or to establish a new arena in the Seattle area.

Unfortunately for Sonics fans, in mid-April 2007, the Washington legislature voted against allocating taxpayer dollars to finance a new arena. As a consequence, Seattle media reported,

---

6. *In re Liebman* at 41.

7. Frank Hughes, *Why Schultz Tuned Out and Sold the Sonics*, special to ESPN. Updated July 21, 2006, at http://sports.espn.go.com/nba/columns/story?columnist =hughes_frank&id=2525634 (last visited March 18, 2013).

8. Berry Tramel, *Investor Group Buys Supersonics*, The Daily Oklahomian, July 19, 2006. *See also* 2nd Amended Complaint, 200 9WL 4464 839, at line 4.5.

Bennett would consider relocating the Sonics before the expiration of the Key Arena lease in 2010.[9]

This forced Bennett into a conundrum: He had to fill the arena for at least the '07–'08 season while he worked through the lease issues. So PBC created and promoted the "Emerald Club," a set of benefits extended to '06–'07 season ticket holders (STHs) to encourage them to renew their tickets for the '07–'08 season.

The Emerald Club Brochure set forth several promises that could almost be interpreted as communicating an offer:

(1) The brochure called this an "unprecedented offer" to Sonics season ticket holders to provide three-year cost certainty—if the STHs renewed their tickets for the '07–'08 season they could pay the '06–'07 price for up to three years.

(2) It included a personal message from Clay Bennett assuring the specific '06–'07 season ticket holders to whom it was mailed that he would keep the team in Seattle despite the much-publicized uncertainty surrounding the lease:

> At a time when we are asking you for your season ticket renewal, it is of paramount importance that we establish our commitment to you, our most passionate and supportive fan. Therefore, we are creating the Sonics Emerald Club, an exclusive membership for current Season Ticket Holders. Sonics Emerald Club members will earn long-term price assurances, enhanced amenities and priority activation related to the new arena.[10]

(3) It listed benefits pertaining to the guaranteed cost certainty:

---

9. Jim Brunner, *Bennett Says He Plans to File Moving Papers*. Deadline for new arena deal: Oct. 31, 2007. Sonics, Storm owner tells Oklahoma paper "he's out of ideas," May 31, 2007, Seattle Times at D4. *See also Brotherson* at 1289.

10. *Brotherson* 604 F. Supp. 2d 1276, 1281.

> Renew your season tickets and earn guaranteed cost certainty through 2009–10.
>
> By renewing your account with a 10% non-refundable deposit by Wednesday, April 25, 2007, your account will be established at 2006–2007 prices. Provided you maintain an active full-season account in good standing through the 2009–10 season, you will receive 2006–07 pricing. If you choose to change seat locations or upgrade your seat status you will pay the 2006–07 price for those seats.
>
> There will be a price increase for new season ticket accounts—but your membership in the exclusive Emerald Club will always differentiate your account status and provide you with price assurance.[11]

But on September 21, 2007—after selling almost 1,400 season tickets for the '07–'08 season through the brochure—Bennett filed a demand for arbitration with the American Arbitration Association to break the lease with the City of Seattle; he then announced his plan to move the team from Seattle to Oklahoma City.

Three incensed STHs who felt duped by the promises in the brochure filed a lawsuit against Bennett for, *inter alia*, breach of contract. They argued that the Emerald Club Brochure was a contract that guaranteed them the right to renew their Seattle season tickets at the '06–'07 price through the '09–'10 NBA season, which they would be unable to do when the team played in Oklahoma City starting in '08.

In ruling on motions for summary judgment, U.S. District Judge Richard A. Jones reviewed the parties' arguments and

---

11. *Brotherson* at 1280.

based his opinion on three factors: (1) whether the Emerald Club Brochure formed a binding contract, (2) whether PBC's defenses to contract formation applied, and (3) whether the brochure included a right to renew.

In determining whether there was a contract for PBC to breach, Judge Jones looked to the basic elements of a contract: offer, acceptance, and consideration.

(1) Offer—The court determined that the brochure contained all the essential terms of an offer:

(a) It called itself an offer;

(b) It defined the persons to whom the offer was open: all '06–'07 season ticket holders;

(c) It stated a fixed price: whatever price the ticket holder paid for '06–'07 tickets;

(d) It stated several material terms with precision; and

(e) It gave precise instructions for accepting the offer, including options for acceptance by telephone, by mail, or on the team's website, as well as three payment options.

(2) Acceptance—The STHs accepted the offer by paying the ticket price pursuant to the brochure's instructions.

(3) Consideration—PBC contended that even if the season ticket holders paid consideration for the '07–'08 season tickets, no separate consideration was paid for the renewal options for the following two years. But the court stated that the law requires no separate consideration for an option contained within a broader contract:

> When an option agreement is a subsidiary part of a larger transaction, as where a party is given an option to renew a contract, the consideration for

the option itself is rarely a definitely determinable portion of what the option holder gives to the other party. The parties need not make a separate valuation of the option in order for it to be enforceable.[12]

As all three defined parts of a contract were present, the judge held that the brochure created a contract.

But PBC argued against contract formation—that there was, in fact, no offeree, and where there's no offeree, there can be no contract.

PBC presented evidence that some STHs failed to read the brochure before renewing. PBC argued that those STHs did not accept the offer and were not subject to a contract.

The court found that the three plaintiffs received and read the contract and that, even if they had not read the contract, as PBC contended, they were given the opportunity to read it and "a party who accepts a written offer without reading it nonetheless objectively manifests his or her assent to its terms."

Even so, the court said, "to the extent that failure to read an offer can ever serve as a defense to contract formation, it is a defense to be invoked by the party who failed to read, not by the party who provided the written offer."

Once he determined that the brochure formed a binding contract, the judge looked to whether it was a contract for a mere license—revocable upon refunding the contract price, as PBC contended, or a contract for the right to renew season tickets for two years—a denial of which would constitute a breach—as the STHs maintained.

PBC made several arguments to support its case that the season tickets constituted revocable licenses and that

---

12. *Brotherson* at 1285 (quoting *Metro Park District v. Griffith*, 106 Wash.2d 425, 23 P2d 1093, 1099 (1986)).

because there was no right to renew them, there was no breach or damages.

PBC claimed:

(1) By definition, a ticket is a license revocable at will;

(2) A reasonable person would have understood that the tickets were licenses revocable at will, as no one would have thought they were purchasing a property interest in a seat in Key Arena;

(3) Given the uncertainty surrounding the Sonics' commitment to stay in Seattle, no specific person could believe that the contract contained an option to renew season tickets after the '07–'08 season;

(4) The ticket-back language specifically said that the tickets were revocable licenses, as did the guide that PBC sent season ticket holders after they entered the contract; and

(5) Remaining in Seattle was an implied condition precedent to the right to renew.

The court wholeheartedly disagreed with each one of those arguments.

As in the *Suns* and *Bulls* cases, the Seattle judge's decision turned on the four corners of the contract. However, in Seattle, the contract omitted key language absent from the ones present in Phoenix and Chicago.

First, in addressing PBC's definition of a ticket, the judge found that PBC *agreed otherwise*—(1) the brochure explicitly promised to fix the price renewals for two years and (2) included no language indicating that the contract was revocable at will.

If PBC intended to sell tickets that could be revoked at any time for any reason, it was obligated to objectively communicate as much in the Emerald Club offer. The judge held that, given the omission of the phrase "revocable at will" in the contract, PBC presented no support for the notion that the revocable nature of the tickets is disclosed within the four corners of the Emerald Club Contract. (You may recall that the contract in the *Bulls* case expressly stated that the tickets were revocable at will.)

Second, the court found unavailing the argument that any reasonable person entering the contract would have understood that the tickets were revocable and did not create a property interest in a seat or access to Key Arena. It found no support for the argument that the common understanding of the term ticket was that of a revocable license. And it reiterated the necessity to look to the four corners of the contract and the significance of the omission of the phrase "revocable at will."

Third, PBC contended that the STHs subjectively believed the Sonics would not stay in Seattle, even though the contract said differently. The court found the subjective beliefs of the parties irrelevant:

> [N]either the subjective or objective doubts of Emerald Club offerees affects the formation of the contract. PBC strays far from contract law by arguing that what Plaintiffs subjectively believed about whether the Sonics would stay in Seattle is relevant. It is not. Even if every person who entered the Emerald Club Contract believed that the Sonics would move at the end of the 2008 season, that belief does not affect the Contract's validity. PBC promised the right to renew season tickets at a fixed price in 2009 and 2010.[13]

Fourth, the judge determined that the extrinsic evidence that PBC proffered hindered PBC's argument, rather than

---

13. *Brotherson* at 1290.

advanced it. The judge examined the differences in the Season Ticketholder Guide and the ticket-back language, and the timing of their distribution to the STHs.

The guide that PBC sent season ticket holders *after* they entered the Emerald Club contract discusses conditions that would permit it to revoke tickets, but *does not state that tickets were revocable at will.* In addition, even if it did have the required language, it was sent *after* the contract was signed.

On the other hand, the tickets themselves, which Emerald Club members received *after* they entered the contract, included the following ticket-back language: "this ticket is a revocable license."

One can infer the legal maxim—*inclusio unius est exclusio alterius*—from the judge's opinion, such that the individual tickets were revocable, because they stated so, but the contract was not, as it failed to make that statement.

The ticket-back language contains a per-game license that does not attach until the ticket holder attends the game. Even if the license is enforceable (an issue not before the court) it gives PBC a single-game right to revoke a ticket after the ticket holder enters the arena for that game, not the ability to revoke all of the tickets under the contract before they are used.

Fifth, the judge found no basis for the argument that the Sonics remaining in Seattle was an implied condition precedent for the right to renew the tickets. PBC did not state in the contract that the cost certainty expressed in the contract depended on the Sonics playing at Key Arena. The judge said that PBC could have easily expressed such a condition by adding a disclaimer that made the renewal option for the '08–'09 and '09–'10 seasons contingent on the Sonics remaining at Key Arena. However, it declined to do so, forfeiting any right to argue that such a condition existed.

To the Hoop 1

Revocable Promises

It would be prudent for a team lawyer to review all of the marketing materials and regularly discuss with ticket sales executives any promises that they make to current and potential ticket holders. The teams would be smart to include disclaimers and "revocable at will" language.

As to the breach of contract cause of action, the court found that the STHs established as a matter of law that the parties entered the Emerald Club contract and that the contract contained two renewal options—one for '08–'09 and one for '09–'10.

However, the court questioned whether the STHs waived their rights to exercise those options and left that question for a jury to decide. If the jury determines that the STHs did not waive their rights, the jury must determine the amount of damages the STH shall receive from PBC's breach of that option contract and whether those damages were within the reasonable expectation of the parties when they entered the Emerald Club contract.

Eventually, the case settled. It was reported that under the settlement terms, about 1,000 former Sonics season ticket holders were to receive $1.6 million from PBC.[14] Alas, the Emerald Club was like the Emerald City: both sparkly visions, but then only illusions.

---

14. The Associated Press, *Clay Bennett Agrees to Pay Former Sonics Ticket Holders $1.6 Million*, Seattle Times, Jan. 21, 2010, at http://seattletimes.com/html/nba/2010857910_soni22.html (last visited March 18, 2013).

Chapter 2

Picking Off Name Brands:

Professional Basketball Players and the Rights to Their Names

Kareem Abdul-Jabbar v. General Motors Corp., 85 F.3d 407 (9th Cir. 1996); *Mine O'Mine, Inc. v. Calmese and True Fan Logo, Inc.*, 2011 WL 2728390 (D. Nev. 2011)

P icture the following dramatization of a television commercial that ran during the 1993 NCAA basketball tournament:

OFF-SCREEN VOICE: "How 'bout some trivia?"

FOLLOWED BY PRINTED WORDS: "You're talking to the champ."

OFF-SCREEN VOICE: "Who holds the record for being voted the most outstanding player of this tournament?"

FOLLOWED BY "THE ANSWER" IN PRINTED WORDS: "Lew Alcindor, UCLA, '67, '68, '69."

OFF-SCREEN VOICE: "Has any car made the 'Consumer Digest's Best Buy' list more than once?"

OFF-SCREEN VOICE RESPONDS: "The Oldsmobile Eighty-Eight has."

CLIP OF: The Olds 88 with its price.

OFF-SCREEN VOICE PLAYS DURING THE CLIP: "In fact, it's made that list three years in a row. And now you can get this Eighty-Eight special edition for just $18,995."

PRINTED WORDS: "A Definite First Round Pick."

ACCOMPANIED BY OFF-SCREEN VOICE: "It's your money."

PRINTED MESSAGE: "Demand Better, 88 by Oldsmobile."

After this commercial aired, former UCLA Bruin and Los Angeles Laker Kareem Abdul-Jabbar filed a lawsuit against General Motors Corporation for violating his trademark and his right of publicity in the name Lew Alcindor—Abdul-Jabbar's birth name—by using it without his permission.

Abdul-Jabbar contended that GM's unauthorized use of his birth name (the Alcindor Mark) was likely to confuse consumers about his endorsement of the Olds 88, and thus use of that name violates the Lanham Act.[1]

To prevail in a trademark infringement suit under the Lanham Act, Abdul-Jabbar needed to prove he had:

(1) a legally protectable mark, including a name, symbol, or other "uniquely distinguishing characteristic" of celebrity identity (the Alcindor Mark in this case);

(2) its use by GM in interstate commerce (a national television commercial in this case); and

(3) a likelihood of confusion as to association or sponsorship with GM's products or services.

GM argued that Abdul-Jabbar did not meet the first prong in that he did not have a legally protectable mark. GM claimed that: (1) Abdul-Jabbar lost his rights to the name Lew Alcindor when he abandoned it by legally changing his name and (2) in

---

1. *Abdul-Jabbar* Appellate Brief, 1994 WL 16506828. *See* Lanham Act 15 USC § 1125 (a).

the alternative, GM's use of the name Lew Alcindor was a nominative fair use that is not subject to the protection of the Lanham Act. The district court ruled both defenses applicable.

It would first help to understand what constitutes a trademark before discussing how it is abandoned.

A trademark is a source identifier. It tells you the source, sponsor, or affiliation of the product or service. A trademark does not stand on its own; it only receives protection for the goods or services with which it is used. For example, Spalding for basketballs, Nike for clothing. When you see those marks you, as the consumer, assume some qualities about those products.

Trademark abandonment means the mark is no longer associated with the owner. It falls into the public domain and is "fair game" for the public to use.

The Lanham Act provides two ways to abandon a mark: (1) non-use with an intent not to resume use, with non-use for two consecutive years being prima facie evidence of abandonment, and (2) the course of conduct of the owner causes the mark to become generic.[2] A prima facie case of abandonment may be rebutted by showing valid reasons for non-use or lack of intent to abandon. Once a mark is abandoned, it may be used by another.

Abdul-Jabbar acknowledged that he had not used the name Lew Alcindor in more than ten years. In fact, he had taken on a new religion and registered his new name under the Illinois name recordation statute.

The U.S. District Court for the Central District of California found these actions proved that Abdul-Jabbar had in effect abandoned his birth name and "the right to protect that name, and the right to assert any other rights that flow from his having

---

2. Lanham Act 15 USC § 1127 (1992).

had that name at one time in the past." Any religious reasons for doing so, the court said, were inapplicable.

The district court held that since Abdul-Jabbar had changed his name and was no longer using his birth name, he had abandoned the Alcindor Mark and had no legally protectable mark in GM's ad.

On appeal, the 9th Circuit rejected GM's abandonment defense. It found that the abandonment defense had never been applied to a "person's name or identity" and declined to stretch federal law to encompass the defense with regard to the use of a person's name.

"One's birth name is an integral part of one's identity; it is not bestowed for commercial purposes, nor is it 'kept alive' through commercial use. A proper name thus cannot be deemed 'abandoned' . . . it will always refer to the person who bore it." Thus, he has a legally protectable right in the Alcindor Mark.

But GM had more than one play drawn up. GM had also argued on the district court level, that even if Abdul-Jabbar still had rights in the name Lew Alcindor, GM only used the Alcindor Mark nominatively. Nominative use is trademark law's version of the fair use defense. It applies where the mark is used merely to describe the good or service. In other words, the only way to refer to the product is to use its name.[3]

Courts in the 9th Circuit apply a three-part test to determine whether a trademark use qualifies for the nominative defense. Under this test from *New Kids On The Block v. New America Pub., Inc.*, 971 F.2d 302 (9th Cir. 1992), for the nominative defense to apply:

(1) the product or service in question must be one not readily identifiable without use of the trademark;

---

3. Lanham Act 15 USC § 1115(b)(4).

(2) only so much of the mark or marks may be used as is reasonably necessary to identify the product or service; and

(3) the user must do nothing that would, in conjunction with the mark, suggest sponsorship or endorsement by the trademark holder.

The district court found for GM on all three prongs as a matter of law.

With the first prong, the district court stated that Abdul-Jabbar's name was not identifiable without actually using the Alcindor Mark. "One might refer to the 'two-time world champions' or 'the professional basketball team from Chicago,' but it's far simpler (and more likely to be understood) to refer to the Chicago Bulls. . . [I]ndeed, it would be impossible to refer to the NCAA record in question without referring to Lew Alcindor."[4]

On the second prong, the district court noted that in *New Kids*, the newspapers satisfied this requirement because they only used the mark and *not any distinctive logo* to make the announcements intelligible to readers. "Similarly, in this case, defendants only used the name in the record book, nothing more. Accordingly, the district court found that defendants used what was reasonably necessary to identify plaintiff as the holder of the record."

As to the third prong, the district court found that, like the newspaper polls in the *New Kids* case, nothing in "The Answer" to the trivia question on the commercial suggest sponsorship or endorsement by the plaintiff.

On appeal, the 9th Circuit agreed with the district court as to prongs 1 and 2 but concluded that there was a genuine

---

4. GM Reply Brief, *Kareem Abdul-Jabbar v. General Motors Corporation*, 1994 WL 16506841 at 8 (C.A. 9) (Appellate Brief) No. 94-55597, Nov. 9, 1994, citing DC# CV-93-02813-IH Central District of California (Los Angeles), Appellees' Brief.

issue of fact as to prong 3. Basically, the panel found that celebrity endorsements on TV are so common that a jury could find Abdul-Jabbar endorsed the Olds 88 by GM's use of his name in its commercial:[5]

> Had GMC limited itself to the "trivia" portion of its ad, GMC could likely defend the reference to Lew Alcindor as a nominative fair use. But by using Alcindor's record to make a claim for its car—like the basketball star, the Olds 88 won an "award" three years in a row, and like the star, the car is a "champ" and a "first round pick"—GMC has arguably attempted to "appropriate the cachet of one product for another," if not also to "capitalize on consumer confusion."

Therefore, the 9th Circuit held whether GM was entitled to a fair use defense was a question of fact.

Once the 9th Circuit determined that Abdul-Jabbar had a legally protectable mark and no defenses applied, it looked to whether there was a likelihood of confusion as to Abdul-Jabbar's association or sponsorship with the GM's products or services.

The 9th Circuit considers the following "likelihood of confusion" factors in determining whether the unauthorized use of a celebrity's name violates the Lanham Act: "(1) strength of the plaintiff's mark; (2) relatedness of the goods; (3) similarity of the marks; (4) evidence of actual confusion; (5) marketing channels used; (6) likely degree of purchaser care; (7) defendant's intent in selecting the mark."

It noted that because a jury could reasonably conclude that most of the factors weighed in Abdul-Jabbar's favor, a jury would need to decide whether a likelihood of confusion exists.

---

5. This was essentially what Abdul-Jabbar argued in his Appellate Brief. *See* 1994 WL 1606828, *Abdul-Jabbar v. General Motors Corp., et.al.*, No. 94-55597, Sept. 21, 1994.

Let's review. The district court found that Abdul-Jabbar had abandoned his birth name and lost his trademark rights in the Alcindor Mark. It alternatively determined that even if Abdul-Jabbar had rights in the Alcindor Mark, GM's use was nominative. On appeal, the 9th Circuit reversed, holding that a person cannot abandon trademark rights in his birth name—thus Abdul-Jabbar had protectable rights in the Alcindor Mark, that GM's nominative use defense was also a question for a jury, and that a jury must balance the likelihood of confusion factors to determine trademark infringement.

Moving on, Abdul-Jabbar had also claimed that GM violated his rights of publicity in the Alcindor Mark.

In addition to trademark rights, an athlete has rights of publicity in his name and likeness.[6] The right of publicity generally refers to the right to control and profit from the commercial use of one's identity. There is no federal right of publicity statute. It is solely recognized through state common law, state statute, or both. California recognizes both.

A right of publicity cause of action under California common law requires: "(1) the defendant's use of plaintiff's identity; (2) the appropriation of plaintiff's name or likeness to defendant's advantage, commercially or otherwise; (3) lack of consent; and (4) resulting injury."[7]

California's common law cause of action is complemented with a right of publicity statute. It provides in pertinent part:

> Any person who knowingly uses another's name, voice, signature, photograph, or likeness, in any manner, on or in products, merchandise, or goods, or for pur-

---

6. *See Haelan Laboratories v. Topps Chewing Gum*, 202 F.2d 866 (2d Cir. 1953).

7. *Kareem Abdul-Jabbar v. General Motors Corporation*, 85 F.3d 407, 413, 414 (9th Cir. 1996) quoting *Eastwood v. Superior Court for Los Angeles County*, 149 Cal. App.3d 409, 198 Cal.Rptr. 342, 347 (1983).

poses of advertising or selling, or soliciting purchases of, products, merchandise, goods or services, without such person's prior consent . . . shall be liable for any damages sustained by the person . . . injured as a result thereof.[8]

The statute requires two more allegations than the common law cause of action. It requires that (1) the defendant knowingly used the other's name or likeness, demonstrating an awareness or intent, and (2) there is a direct connection between use and a commercial purpose, meaning that if the name is not used commercially, the use would not fall under the statute.

Under both causes of action, California does not require the plaintiff to show that the use of his or her name or picture suggests an endorsement or association with the product or service. Unlike trademarks, mere use is actionable, as opposed to use that causes consumer confusion in the endorsement or sponsorship. Abdul-Jabbar did not need to show that the use of his name was likely to confuse the public regarding his endorsement of the Olds 88 for his right of publicity claim to succeed.

Abdul-Jabbar therefore argued that GM violated his right of publicity under California common law and the statute when it used his birth name in its commercial for the Olds 88 without his consent.

The district court found that GM was entitled to summary judgment on both rights of publicity causes of action. It ruled that because Abdul-Jabbar had abandoned the Lew Alcindor name, GM was not using the plaintiff's name, since at the time of use, Lew Alcindor was no longer his name.

The 9th Circuit disagreed with the district court yet again.

---

8. Cal. Civil Code § 3344(a) (1971).

It gave two reasons why Abdul-Jabbar's right of publicity claims could proceed under both California common law and the statute.

For one, since both causes of action omit the word "present" prior to the words "identity" and "name," the "identity" or "name" could be a past moniker. It ruled that GM's unauthorized use of Abdul-Jabbar's birth name was actionable because at one time Lew Alcindor was his name, even though it wasn't his then-current name. Second, a celebrity's decision not to exploit his name commercially does not preclude the celebrity from enforcing his rights against its unauthorized use by others. Just because Abdul-Jabbar didn't exploit his birth name, didn't mean that GM could.

The 9th Circuit reversed the district court, holding that Abdul-Jabbar's right of publicity claims could also proceed.

Nearly fifteen years after Abdul-Jabbar prevailed against GM, on January 12, 2010, Shaquille O'Neal filed a trademark suit against Michael D. Calmese and his company, True Logo Fan, Inc., for registering without O'Neal's consent, the domain name "shaqtus.net" and selling clothing with the logo of a basketball-playing cactus wearing a number 32 jersey.[9]

It all started in February 2008, when the Miami Heat had traded O'Neal to the Phoenix Suns. In Phoenix, O'Neal wore an orange jersey with the number 32. Sportswriters began referring to him as "The Shaqtus," "The Big Cactus," and "The Big Shaqtus." In addition, ESPN aired commercials with O'Neal encountering a cactus with O'Neal's face in the Arizona desert.

Shortly thereafter, Calmese registered the domain name shaqtus.net with GoDaddy.com and the trade name "Shaqtus" with the Arizona Secretary of State. In addition, Calmese hired

---

9. *Mine o'Mine, Inc. v. True Fan Logo, Inc.*, 2010 WL 2068926 (Complaint).

an artist to create his "Shaqtus," a basketball-playing cactus—with the facial expression of a man—wearing an orange basketball jersey bearing the name "Phoenix Shaqtus" and the number 32 (the Shaqtus Character). Calmese sold clothing with the Shaqtus trade name and Shaqtus Character online at Shaqtus.net.

To recap, Calmese's company used a variation of Shaq as its web address, where it sold T-shirts bearing an eerily familiar-looking character with the name Phoenix Shaqtus printed on them.

Did O'Neal have any valid claims against Calmese for using the term Shaqtus and an arguably imitation basketball player? He certainly thought so and so did the U.S. district court in Nevada.

After first sending Calmese a cease-and-desist letter,[10] O'Neal sued Calmese and his company, claiming six causes of action, two of which will be discussed here: trademark infringement under the Lanham Act and violation of O'Neal's rights of publicity in the Shaq Character.

O'Neal's success on the court is well-known. He played basketball at Louisiana State University from 1990–92. Then, the Orlando Magic selected him as the number-one pick in the 1992 National Basketball Association rookie draft. He went on to win three consecutive NBA Championships (2000, 2001, 2002) with the Los Angeles Lakers and a fourth title with the Miami Heat (2006). O'Neal played for Phoenix, Cleveland, and Boston, and retired from the NBA in 2011 and shortly after joined TNT's

---

10. Initially, Calmese sent a letter to ESPN claiming he was part-owner of the Shaqtus trademark and that ESPN's commercial causes a likelihood of confusion with his rights. He offered to enter into a business arrangement with ESPN. ESPN responded that MOM owns the Shaq mark and had given ESPN permission to use it, to which Calmese responded that he, not MOM, owns the Shaqtus mark. Shortly thereafter, counsel for MOM sent Calmese a letter demanding he and his company cease and desist from all use of the Shaqtus mark, to transfer <Shaqtus.net> to MOM, and to cancel his Arizona trade name registration for Shaqtus. 2010 WL 2068926 (D. Nev.) (Trial Pleading), United States District Court, D. Nev., *Mine O'Mine Inc., v. Calmese*, No. 10CV00043, Jan. 12, 2010.

"Inside the NBA." Sportswriters nicknamed him Shaq early in his career.

What may not be as well-known as his basketball record is his business acumen. In 1993, O'Neal founded the company Mine O' Mine, Inc. (MOM), of which he is the president, secretary, and treasurer. He granted MOM the exclusive right to sublicense his name, image, and likeness and to register, exploit, and protect the word "Shaq" and Shaq formative marks including, among others: Shaq, Shaqtacular, Shaq Attaq, and Shaq's All Star Comedy Jam. Under his direction, MOM registered several SHAQ trademarks with the United States Patent and Trademark Office.

As the *Abdul-Jabbar* case showed, to prevail on a claim of trademark infringement under the Lanham Act, the trademark owner must prove: (1) that it has a protectable ownership interest in the mark and (2) that the defendant's use of the mark is likely to cause consumer confusion.

Calmese did not contest MOM's U.S. trademark registrations for the Shaq and Shaq formative marks, but questioned whether the use of the mark Shaqtus caused a likelihood of confusion.

The district court considered eight factors to determine the likelihood of consumer confusion: "(1) strength of the mark; (2) proximity of the goods; (3) similarity of the marks; (4) evidence of actual confusion; (5) marketing channels used; (6) type of goods and the degree of care likely to be exercised by the purchaser; (7) defendant's intent in selecting the mark; and (8) likelihood of expansion of the product lines."

1. Strength of the Mark

In analyzing whether likelihood of confusion exists, the court first looked to the strength of the mark. The stronger the mark, the more likely the public will associate it with the trademark owner. There are two indicators of strength: conceptual and commercial strength.

The mark's "conceptual strength" refers to where the mark lies on the spectrum of distinctiveness. There are four degrees of distinctiveness.

A generic mark is afforded no protection because it simply names a product, such as, "chair" for chair. A descriptive mark also does not receive protection, because it merely describes a product, for example, "gift card." However, once a descriptive mark obtains secondary meaning, it receives protection. Secondary meaning is the public's association of that term with a source.

Then, there is a suggestive mark, which suggests a quality or characteristic of the goods and services. A suggestive mark requires some imagination or thought to reach a conclusion about the nature of the goods, while a descriptive mark allows one to reach that conclusion without such imagination.

An arbitrary mark is afforded more protection; and a fanciful mark, which is a wholly made-up term, receives the maximum protection. In addition, "a federal trademark registration of a particular mark supports the distinctiveness of that mark."

Second, a mark's "commercial strength" is indicated based on "actual marketplace recognition" of the mark and the absence of third-party uses of a mark.

The court found the Shaq mark exhibited both conceptual and commercial strength: conceptually strong because it is a coined term that does not exist in the English language, and commercially strong because it has been used nationwide since the 1990s to refer to O'Neal and goods or services that originate with him or his company.

The court said: "It can hardly be disputed that any sports fan who has lived in the United States or watched the NBA in at least the past fifteen years would conclude that a reference to 'Shaq' is a reference to O'Neal." This factor weighed in favor of O'Neal.

Two points for Shaq.

2. Proximity of the Goods

Proximity of goods refers to the relatedness of the goods at issue. The proximity of goods is measured by whether the products are (1) complementary; (2) sold to the same class of purchasers; and (3) similar in use and function.

The court looked at the fact that both MOM and Calmese sold T-shirts with the Shaqtus mark. It determined that "[t]he shirts are complementary because they are both shirts that reference the same NBA player. There are no different classes of T-shirt consumers, and T-shirts with the Shaq mark are identical in use and function as T-shirts with the Shaqtus mark." This factor weighs in favor of finding a likelihood of confusion.

Two more points for Shaq.

3. Similarity of the Marks

The court looked to the sight, sound, and meaning of the marks to judge their similarity.

It noted that both the Shaqtus mark and the Shaq marks begin with the same four letters. "[W]hen consumers read and hear the two terms, Shaqtus and Shaq, they see and hear words that are similar in sight and sound. Further, since Shaq and Shaqtus have both been used to refer to O'Neal, the marks are similar in meaning."

Additionally, the court applied the family of marks doctrine. Under that doctrine, a trademark owner may use and own several marks with a common prefix, similar to a surname. It found that MOM owns a family of marks containing the surname Shaq, including Shaq, ShaqTACULAR, and Shaq ATTAQ.

"The Shaqtus mark also contains the Shaq surname. Therefore, Shaqtus clearly falls within the scope of MOM's family of marks. Accordingly, this factor weighs in favor of finding a likelihood of confusion."

Two more points for Shaq.

4. Evidence of Actual Confusion

Actual confusion would occur when a computer user visited Shaqtus.net expecting to see merchandise licensed by the real Shaquille O'Neal. Actual confusion is not necessary for likelihood of confusion. Although it would weigh on the likelihood side, as neither party submitted facts to support or dispel actual confusion the court did not consider this factor in its analysis.

A draw.

5. Marketing Channels Used

The court noted that usually similar marketing channels increase the likelihood of confusion. However, when the marketing channel is the Internet, since nearly all retailers advertise online, this factor is hardly telling. Since the only marketing channel MOM and Calmese shared was the Internet, the court concluded that although it leaned toward O'Neal, "the actual importance of this factor is minuscule."

One point for Shaq.

6. Type of Goods and the Degree of Care Likely to Be Exercised by the Purchaser

"Low consumer care . . . increases the likelihood of confusion . . . When the goods at issue are inexpensive, consumers are less likely to exercise much care in making purchasing decisions."

The court found that because "T-shirts are inexpensive and consumers exercise little care when deciding to buy a T-shirt, this factor weighs in favor of finding a likelihood of confusion."

For example, consumers will see the mark "Shaq" on a shirt and make a quick purchase, rather than contemplate whether it is the "real Shaq."

Two more points for Shaq.

7. Intent in Selecting the Mark

When the alleged infringer knowingly adopts a mark similar to another's mark, courts presume an intent to deceive the public and that intent is strong evidence of a likelihood of confusion.

The court easily found that Calmese intended to cause confusion with the Shaqtus mark, as he knew about the Shaq mark and chose "Shaqtus" only after O'Neal was traded to the Phoenix Suns.

Two more points for Shaq.

8. Likelihood of Expansion of the Product Lines

The court looked at the likelihood of Calmese expanding his product lines to overlap with additional Shaq goods and services. Normally, the fact that both parties sell the same goods would lean in favor of a likelihood of confusion. However, in the current scenario, the court found this factor did not weigh in favor of a likelihood of confusion since O'Neal no longer plays for the Phoenix Suns and a Shaqtus T-shirt lacks marketability. Further, Calmese asserted that he is not presently selling Shaqtus gear. The likelihood of expansion therefore is low.

Two points for Calmese.

If you are keeping score, that was 11 out of 16 points for O'Neal and 2 out of 16 points for Calmese.

So as to the trademark claim, the court found that the facts showed: (1) that MOM has a protectable ownership interest in the Shaq and Shaq formative marks and (2) that Calmese's use of the Shaqtus mark was likely to cause consumer confusion.

To the Hoop 2

Name and Fame

Professional basketball players continue to benefit from the trademarks in their names and their rights of publicity—significantly. Forbes.com reported in January 2012[1] that Kobe Bryant makes $28 million annually from endorsing Nike, Smart Car, Panini, and Turkish Airlines. LeBron James makes $33 million annually through partnerships with Nike, Coca-Cola, McDonald's, State Farm, and Upper Deck. Dwight Howard makes $11 million annually from sponsors like Adidas and McDonald's. However, as offenders still attempt to cash in on the cachet of a basketball player's name *absent consent*, star athletes have a growing body of case law to support their rights.

1. *See* http://www.forbes.com/sites/kurtbadenhausen/2012/01/25/the-top-earning-nba-players/.

Accordingly, it found no genuine issues of material fact and granted MOM judgment as a matter of law on its trademark infringement claims.

On the other hand, the court denied O'Neal relief on his claim under the Nevada right of publicity statute.

Nevada's right of publicity statute states, in part:

Any commercial use by another of the name, voice, signature, photograph or likeness of a person requires the written consent of that person or his or her successor in interest . . . .[11]

O'Neal argued that the use of the Shaqtus Character on the shirts violated his rights of publicity in his name and likeness.

The district court in Nevada looked to how the 9th Circuit

11. Nev. Rev. Stat. Section 597.790.

addresses right of publicity cases when cartoons depict real people. It found that the 9th Circuit uses the transformative use test when cartoons depicting real persons are "distorted for purposes of lampoon, parody, or caricature." The 9th Circuit had held that "'half-human and half worm' characters . . . were sufficiently transformative to defeat a right of publicity action brought by the entirely human persons on which they were based."

Applying that reasoning, since the Shaqtus Character was half-human and half-cactus, the district court in Nevada found Calmese's use of the Shaqtus Character was sufficiently transformative to defeat a right of publicity cause of action.

In addition, the district court did not afford a nickname the same rights of publicity as the 9th Circuit bestowed on a birth name. The court stated: "Further, Shaqtus is not O'Neal's real name, voice or signature and thus is not protected by Nev. Rev. Stat. § 597.790.1."

Accordingly, the court dismissed the right of publicity claim. All's not necessarily fair in cars and cacti.

Chapter 3

Boxing Out Potential Owners:
Contentious Team Sales

Levin v. NBA, 385 F. Supp. 149 (S.D.N.Y. 1974)

I n 1972, movie producer Irving Levin and lawyer Harold Lipton signed an agreement to purchase the Boston Celtics from its owner, the Ballantine Brewing Company. All they needed was a sign-off from the NBA approving the sale. However, the NBA does not rubber-stamp transfers of ownership—NBA rules require an affirmative vote from three-quarters of the Board of Governors to approve a transfer of ownership. But, can the NBA reject the sale of a team?

The NBA is organized as a joint venture and operates through its board, which is comprised of one governor as designated by each member team. The board rejected the sale (two votes in favor, thirteen opposed, and one not present) to Levin and Lipton, who immediately requested a personal hearing before the board. After their presentation, another vote was taken, producing the same result.

Feeling (and actually being) rejected, Levin and Lipton sold their rights in the Celtics elsewhere[1] and filed an antitrust action against the NBA in the Southern District of New York.

---

1. *See* James Quirk and Rodney D. Fort, *Pay Dirt: The Business of Professional Team Sports.*

They claimed that the NBA violated Section 1 of the Sherman Act (which prohibits agreements that illegally restrain trade) by preventing them from purchasing the Celtics. They believed that the board's vote was the agreement and the refusal to deal with them as future owners was an illegal restraint of trade. Not surprisingly, the NBA filed a motion for summary judgment requesting the case be dismissed.

Levin and Lipton argued that their friendship with Sam Schulman, the owner of the Seattle SuperSonics, was the reason that the other owners would not deal with them.

Levin testified in a deposition what he recalled then-commissioner Walter Kennedy told him:

> I don't have to draw you a picture. You guys are friendly with Sam Schulman. He is a pain in the neck to the league, and they are obviously worried that if you fellows are also owners, that you will side with Sam Schulman in all matters in the future and cause the league more troubles than they now have with Sam as it is.

Levin also testified that Richard Bloch, then-president of the Phoenix Suns and chairman of the NBA finance committee, told him:

> You are with Sam Schulman. He has been a craw in the throat of these owners. He is a renegade and a rebel, a troublemaker, and he just doesn't play their game, and they are obviously worried that you fellows, being close to Sam, are going to be siding with him on any matters that come up before the NBA.

However, the NBA stated that a business association with Schulman, not a mere friendship, violated the conflict of interest provision of the NBA constitution. That provision reads: "A member shall not exercise control, directly or indirectly, over any other member of the Association." The NBA argued that such a provision is necessary "because there is in fact, and the public believes there is intense competition in the league framework between the teams operated by the N.B.A. members."

In support of the NBA's argument, the San Francisco team listed Levin's and Lipton's specific business conflicts of interest with Schulman:

(1) At the time of the case, Lipton and Levin were shareholders and officers of First Northwest Industries of America, Inc., of which Schulman was the president and principal shareholder;

(2) Levin, Lipton, and Schulman were all officers and employees of the National General Corporation and worked in the same office; and

(3) Lipton had been Schulman's personal attorney for a number of years and, on occasion, provided counsel to Levin as well.

The court conceded that athletic leagues are subject to antitrust laws and that joint action by team members can have antitrust implications. The court held, however, that the board's rejection of the movie producer did not implicate the Sherman Act.

The court said that an antirust violation requires an injury to competition. Here, the court found there was no injury to competition, instead finding that Levin and Lipton merely wanted to join those unwilling to accept them (the NBA), not because they (Levin and Lipton) wanted to compete with them. (Think, *Mean Girls.*)

None of the purported reasons for the rejection were anti-competitive. Even if there was some financial impact on Levin

To the Hoop 3

The Owner as Producer

Irving Levin, who died in 1996, was the producer of
To Live and Die In L.A. and *Hell to Eternity*; and executive
producer on *Eighteen and Anxious; Crashout; and Mivtsa
Yonatan*, a dramatization of the Israeli commando raid
in Entebbe in 1976.

and Lipton from the exclusion, their rejection from league membership did not have an anticompetitive effect, or any effect on the public interest. So, yes, the NBA can reject a sale, at least where the rejection does not affect competition. The court pointed out that the Celtics continued as a club and were even that year's champion. A few years later, Levin and Lipton bought the Celtics and had their Hollywood ending . . . sort of. (See Chapter Four.)

Chapter 4

Double Team:
Two Teams, One City

NBA v. SDC Basketball Club, Inc.,
815 F.2d 562 (9th Cir. 1987)

rving Levin and Harold Lipton, having eventually purchased the Boston Celtics, traded the Celtics for ownership of the Buffalo Braves, which they moved to San Diego in 1978.

By 1984, the team, now known as the Clippers, was ready to leave San Diego for smoggier pastures. They had lost a bunch of games, the arena was in disrepair,[1] they believed the Los Angeles population could sustain two teams,[2] and they hoped L.A. would give them some R-E-S-P-E-C-T.[3]

The Oakland Raiders gave them *all the right moves* to get there. So before we can delve into the story behind the Clippers move, we need to discuss that of the Raiders.

Al Davis, owner of the Oakland Raiders football team from 1972 until his death in 2011, wanted to move his team from the Bay Area to Los Angeles in 1980, over the NFL's objections.

At the time, the NFL Constitution had Rule 4.3, which stated:

---

1. At about the same time they moved, the Clippers were awarded nearly $500,000 by a superior court judge who ruled that the Sports Arena had not been properly maintained. *See* Chris Cobbs, *No One Seemed to Care Much When They Left, But Now . . . DOES SAN DIEGO MISS THE CLIPPERS?* Los Angeles Times, Jan. 27, 1985. Available in 1985 WLNR 975634.

2. *Clippers Moving to Los Angeles*, New York Times, May 16, 1984, at B12. Available in 1984 WLNR 556754.

3. Roy S. Johnson, *All the Right Moves for Clippers?* New York Times, Nov. 1, 1984, at B17. Available in 1984 WLNR 492959.

41

The League shall have exclusive control of the exhibition of football games by member clubs within the home territory of each member. No member club shall have the right to transfer its franchise or playing site to a different city, whether within or outside its home territory, without prior approval by the affirmative vote of ¾'s of the existing member clubs. (*Los Angeles Memorial Coliseum Comm'n v. National Football League*, 726 F.2d 1381, 1384 (9th Cir. 1984).) ("*Raiders I*")

When the other owners voted down his request to move the team (22–0, with 5 abstentions), Davis sued the NFL in the Central District of California on antitrust grounds.

After a jury determined that Rule 4.3 was an unreasonable restraint on trade and found in favor of Davis and the Raiders' move to L.A., the NFL appealed to the 9th Circuit. The 9th Circuit bifurcated the case to decide the liability first (*Raiders I*), and the damages second (*Los Angeles Memorial Coliseum Comm'n v. National Football League*, 791 F.2d 1356 (9th Cir. 1986).) ("*Raiders II*")

As you may recall from Chapter Three, Section 1 of the Sherman Act prohibits a conspiracy or combination in restraint of trade. Davis argued that the NFL clubs' agreement (by a vote) to deny the Raiders' move to L.A., constituted an illegal restraint of trade.

Raiders I pointed out that courts use one of two ways to analyze a Section 1 claim:

(1) They may evaluate whether the conduct constitutes a per se violation: "Agreements among competitors, i.e., cartels, to fix prices or divide market territories are presumed illegal under Section 1 because they give the competitors the ability to charge unreasonable and arbitrary prices instead of setting prices by virtue of free market forces."

(2) Courts may also apply a rule of reason analysis, in which they weigh the procompetitive benefits of the challenged conspiracy or agreement against its anticompetitive effects. Rule of reason is used to "analy[ze] the negative and positive effects of a business practice on an industry that does not readily fit into the antitrust context."

Due to the unique nature of sports leagues, courts generally apply the latter reasoning in sports scenarios. In Davis's case, the 9th Circuit applied a rule of reason analysis to weigh the harms and benefits to competition caused by Rule 4.3 and to determine whether the NFL's proffered benefits could be achieved by less restrictive means.

According to the 9th Circuit, the exclusive territories created by Rule 4.3 embody the harms to competition. They insulate each team from competition, which could lead to set prices, to the detriment of the consuming public. Specifically, the NFL rule would restrict competition between the Rams, who at that time were playing in Anaheim, and the Raiders. (The Rams moved to St. Louis prior to the start of the 1995 season.)

The NFL had argued that Rule 4.3 was merely an "ancillary restraint" to the legitimate purpose of producing NFL football— that it aids the league and that benefits were bountiful:

> . . . in determining its overall geographical scope, regional balance, and coverage of major and minor markets. Exclusive territories aid new franchises in achieving financial stability, which protects the large initial investment an owner must make to start up a football team. Stability arguably helps to ensure that no one team has an undue advantage on the field. Territories foster fan loyalty, which in turn promotes traditional rivalries between teams, each contributing to attendance at games and television viewing.

Therefore, any *side effect* Rule 4.3 had on competition did not violate the Sherman Act.

Generally, the ancillary restraint doctrine is a defense to an antitrust cause of action and permits a restraint on trade that is subordinate or collateral to another legitimate purpose (producing NFL football in this case), *provided* there are no less restrictive means.

The *Raiders I* court found that the competitive harms that the NFL's Rule 4.3 brought about could be avoided if the legitimate goals of Rule 4.3 were achieved through less restrictive means, such as incorporating objective standards to guide a voting decision. These standards could include a city's population, economic projections, playing facilities, regional balance, and television revenues.

So, on February 28, 1984, the 9th Circuit affirmed the jury verdict in favor of Al Davis. It held that it *was reasonable for a jury*, applying the rule of reason analysis, to find that the NFL violated antitrust laws in denying the Raiders' move from Oakland to L.A.

A couple of months later, on May 14, 1984, the San Diego Clippers announced that they too planned to move to Los Angeles—the very next day.

The then-existing NBA rule governing the transfer of franchises was similar to the NFL rule. Armed with the *Raiders I* decision, the Clippers indicated that if the NBA were to prevent their move, they too would bring an antitrust suit challenging the franchise relocation rule.

So, instead of penalizing the Clippers or otherwise preventing or investigating their move, the NBA scheduled the Clippers' subsequent games in L.A.

The NBA, however, made its move as well. The league filed a declaratory judgment action in the U.S. District Court for the

Southern District of California. The NBA sought the court's okay for it to restrain the movement of the Clippers from San Diego to L.A. and to impose a charge on them for the unilateral usurpation of the "franchise opportunity" in the L.A. market.

The NBA argued:

(1) that it could as a league consider the Clippers' move to L.A. and sanction the Clippers for failing to seek league approval;

(2) that the Clippers had breached their fiduciary duty to the other members of the league, and breached their contract with the league to receive league approval for a franchise move; and

(3) the L.A. Coliseum should pay damages to the NBA for tortious interference with the contractual relations between the Clippers and the NBA.

In response, the Clippers counterclaimed against the NBA and the other member teams asserting that any investigation by the NBA of the Clippers' move would violate antitrust laws.

Without issuing a written opinion, the district court suggested that the *Raiders I* result controlled the decision.[4] Accordingly, on April 28, 1986, it entered an order granting summary judgment to the Clippers. It dismissed all of the NBA's claims.

It appeared as though the Clippers were free to play in their own *L.A. Story.*

But, in the interim, the NFL was back in court with the Raiders haggling over damages (*Raiders II*).

The jury had determined that the NFL owed the Raiders

---

4. *NBA v. SDC Basketball Club, Inc.*, 815 F.2d 562, 565 (9th Cir. 1987): "after voluminous pleading and the denial of five summary judgment motions, the district judge suggested on the eve of trial that the NBA could not possibly win its case under the guidelines established in *Raiders I* . . . The district judge also refused NBA counsel's request for a written opinion."

$11.55 million and the Los Angeles Coliseum $4.86 million in damages, to be trebled.

The NFL appealed, asking for damages for the "expansion opportunity" lost to the league by the Raiders' move to Los Angeles. The NFL believed the other member teams should receive remuneration for the L.A. expansion opportunity. If a new team were established in L.A., the existing member clubs would have shared in the initiation fee the new team would have paid to the league. By moving the Raiders from Oakland to L.A., Davis snatched the opportunity without paying for it.

The 9th Circuit agreed with the NFL that the expansion opportunity had a value that the Raiders obtained for free. It therefore offset the Raiders' antitrust award with the value of the franchise opportunity. One more thing to note regarding the *Raiders II* decision: It limited the *Raiders I* relocation analysis to the NFL. You will see why that is important in a minute.

The *Raiders II* decision was issued after the district court dismissed the NBA's action against the Clippers, but *before* the NBA appealed that decision.

With the *Raiders II* decision in its pocket, the NBA had good reason to merrily go back to court. In its appeal, it asked the 9th Circuit for the same two things it initially asked the district court: (1) that it may evaluate and assess limits on franchise movement without violating antitrust laws—the Clippers contended that even the consideration by the NBA of a charge upon the move would violate antitrust laws and (2) that it may charge the Clippers a fee for their unilateral usurpation of the L.A. franchise opportunity.

The 9th Circuit agreed. In adjudicating the appeal in the *Clippers* case, it decided that neither of the *Raiders* opinions held that a franchise movement rule was per se invalid under the antitrust laws. Although it agreed with the holding of *Raid-*

ers I—that a sports franchise relocation rule is subject to a rule of reason analysis—it noted that *Raiders I* was specifically limited to the facts of that case.

The *Clippers* court noted that the court in *Raiders I* had examined the relevant market for professional football, the history, and the purpose of the NFL's franchise movement rule and the NFL's lack of justification for the rule. The *Raiders I* court had found that those facts supported the jury's verdict that the NFL's franchise relocation rule violated the Sherman Act.

But the *Clippers* court read this to mean that any franchise movement rule must be tied to the facts—just because the NFL rule violated the Sherman Act didn't necessarily mean the NBA rule did as well. The *Clippers* court emphasized that what restraints are reasonable is a question of fact, and that each case must be reviewed based on its specific facts.

So in round two of the *Battle [for] Los Angeles*, the Clippers believed the facts were on their side. They argued that the NBA three-quarters rule on franchise movement was illegal under *Raiders I* because the NBA rule did not include "objective standards and criteria, such as population, economic projections, playing facilities, regional balance, and television revenues," which, as *Raiders I* suggested, would make the rule less restrictive.

The *Clippers* court disagreed. Putting aside the fact that the NBA argued that those standards were incorporated into its rule, the *Clippers* court held that the factors listed by the *Raiders I* court were merely guidelines. They were not the sole requirements needed for a rule to avoid antitrust liability. And because the NBA's rule arguably did not have those guidelines, the court said it could not determine on summary judgment that the NBA's rule violated the Sherman Act. There would need to be a factual inquiry as to whether the NBA's rule was reasonable.

To the Hoop 4

Thank You, Davis, Levin, and Lipton

The Clippers' relocation battle with the NBA followed the legal footsteps of the Raiders' with the NFL. The Clippers can thank Al Davis, then, for his feud with the NFL as it set in motion their plans to move to LA. And, the NBA can thank the Clippers as their case gave the OK for the NBA to review a planned move. While we are giving thanks, the NBA can also thank Levin and Lipton for unintentionally having the NBA's right to evaluate a sale recognized. The NBA's relocation rule, as it stands today, requires a simple majority approval of the Board of Governors while the sale of a franchise requires a three-fourths majority.

What is the process when a team wants to sell and relocate?

In January 2013, hedge fund manager Chris Hanson and Microsoft CEO Steve Ballmer announced plans to buy the Sacramento Kings from the Maloof family and move the team to Seattle as the revived SuperSonics.[1]

To the proposed move, the NBA stated: "Two committees would typically vet both the proposed sale and the move of the franchise to Seattle, but [Commissioner David] Stern said he has combined the committees into one. The committee will report to the Board of Governors, which is expected to vote on both the sale and the proposed move at its meeting in mid-April."[2]

If the Kings' relocation to Seattle succeeds, Seattle fans can also thank the late Al Davis and the NBA can thank the Clippers for the chance to review it.

---

1. Ken Belson and Howard Beck, *Seattle Investor Plans to Buy the Kings and Move Them*, Jan. 21, 2013, http://www.nytimes.com/2013/01/22/sports/basket ball/maloof-family-selling-sacramento-kings-to-seattle-investor.html?_r=0 (last visited March 18, 2013).

2. *Stern Says Seattle Group Has Filed for Relocation*, posted Feb. 6, 2013, 7:46 p.m. Updated Feb. 7, 2013, 12:02 a.m. http://www.nba.com/2013/news/02/06/seattle-group-files-for-relocation.ap/index.html (last visited March 18, 2013).

The *Clippers* court thus held that the mere requirement that a team seek NBA approval before it relocates does not by itself violate the Sherman Act. With that, it reversed the district court's dismissal of the NBA's action to the extent that it held that a sports league franchise movement rule is a per se violation of the Sherman Act.

The NBA also wanted the Clippers to pay for the L.A. franchise opportunity, just as the Raiders were required to pay the NFL in *Raiders II*. But the *Clippers* court drew a different conclusion:

> The majority in *Raiders II*, however, found only that the expansion opportunity taken by the Raiders in their move to Los Angeles limited the Raiders' recovery of antitrust damages. The majority revealed nothing about the origin of that offset. Therefore, the *existence* of a recovery for expansion opportunity must find its source somewhere other than antitrust law: i.e., the express or implied provisions of the NBA constitution.[5]

It reversed and remanded, sending the district court on a fact-finding mission to determine:

(1) the purpose of the restraint as demonstrated by the NBA's use of a variety of criteria in evaluating franchise movement;

(2) the differences between the market of professional basketball and that of professional football; and

(3) the actual effect that the limitations movements might have on the trade.

But the district court never fact-found, as the case was settled—the Clippers agreed to pay for the right to remain in L.A.[6]

---

5. *National Basketball Ass'n v. SDC Basketball Club*, 815 F.2d 562, 569.

6. Paul C. Weiler, Gary R. Roberts, Roger J. Abrams & Stephen F. Ross, *Sports and the Law, Text, cases and problems, (4th ed. 2011)* American Casebook Series, at 620.

Chapter 5

Ejected:
Is the NCAA a State Player?

Nat'l Collegiate Athletic Ass'n v. Tarkanian,
488 U.S. 179 (1988); *but see Cohane v. Nat'l Collegiate
Athletic Ass'n,* 215 F. App'x 13 (2d Cir. 2007)

The year before Coach Jerry Tarkanian was hired by the University of Nevada, Las Vegas, its basketball team's won/loss record was 14–14. Within four years of Tarkanian's taking the coaching helm, UNLV's record improved to 29-3, and the Runnin' Rebels placed third in the 1977 NCAA Championship. He is considered a pretty good coach.

But this pretty good coach got stuck in a pretty not so good situation. The NCAA investigated UNLV and found that the university had committed thirty-eight rule violations, including ten recruiting violations by Tarkanian (the most serious of which was Tark's failure to fully cooperate with the NCAA investigation). So, the NCAA requested that UNLV do its own investigation of Tarkanian.

The school obliged, but found no wrongdoing by its beloved coach. Nonetheless, based on its own investigation, the NCAA imposed a number of sanctions against UNLV, including a two-year probation on post-season participation and a ban on television appearances. Moreover, the NCAA told UNLV "to show cause why additional penalties should not be imposed if [UNLV] failed to suspend Tarkanian from its athletic program during a probation period."

UNLV decided it was in the best interest of the school to adhere to the NCAA's warning and suspend Tarkanian from the Rebels basketball program. Tarkanian, however, did not believe a demotion and drastic pay cut were in his best interest. Consequently, he sued UNLV and the NCAA in Nevada state court for depriving him of his due process rights under the U.S. Constitution.

The Fourteenth Amendment provides that no state shall "deprive any person of life, liberty, or property, without due process of law." (U.S. Const. amend. XIV.)

Basically, Tarkanian claimed that UNLV and the NCAA took away his job (a property interest) and prospects to search for a new one (a liberty interest) without any real chance to explain himself, which it couldn't do under the U.S. Constitution.

Only a state actor needs to provide due process. There was no question that UNLV, which is a state-funded university, was a state actor. So the question was whether the NCAA's participation in the events that led to Tarkanian's suspension constituted state action.

The trial court found for Tarkanian. It enjoined UNLV from taking disciplinary action against him and enjoined the NCAA from taking any further action against UNLV. In addition, the trial court required the NCAA to pay Tarkanian's attorney's fees.

On appeal, the Nevada Supreme Court found that the NCAA's conduct turned into state action when the university delegated its authority over personnel decisions to the NCAA by imposing the NCAA sanctions against Tarkanian, and when the NCAA conducted its investigation. The Nevada Supreme Court permitted sanctions against UNLV, but enjoined disciplinary action against Tarkanian.[1]

---

1. *Tarkanian v. Nat'l Collegiate Athletic Ass'n*, 103 Nev. 331, 337, 741 P.2d 1345 (Nev. Sup. Ct. 1987).

The NCAA filed a petition for certiorari with the U.S. Supreme Court. (Notably, UNLV did not challenge the adverse decision.) By the time the U.S. Supreme Court heard the question of whether the NCAA acted under color of state law when it "requested" UNLV to suspend Tarkanian—ten years had passed. Because the trial court's injunction was still in effect, Tarkanian was still coaching basketball at UNLV. Not only that, he had transformed UNLV basketball into a Las Vegas headliner. (See HBO film, *Running Rebels*.)

Justice John Paul Stevens, delivering the 6-3 opinion of the Court, emphasized that the Fourteenth Amendment distinguishes between state action and private conduct ". . . against which the Amendment affords no shield, no matter how unfair that conduct may be."[2]

Tarkanian had argued to the Court that the NCAA was a state actor because UNLV delegated its own functions to the NCAA, permitting the NCAA to adopt rules governing UNLV's athletic programs and enforcing those rules on UNLV's behalf.

The Court examined the typical situation where a private entity acts under the color of state law: the state promulgates a rule and the private party carries it out. Here, the private party created the rule and the state carried it out. So the situation is the reverse of the typical case.

The Court conceded that UNLV was influenced by the rules and recommendations of the NCAA when it carried out the suspension, but it questioned whether that influence was enough to bring the NCAA into the auspices of being a state actor.

First, the Court noted that several hundred public and private NCAA member institutions—most from outside Nevada—created the NCAA's rules, so UNLV had a minor role in helping

---

2. *Nat'l Collegiate Athletic Ass'n v. Tarkanian*, 488 U.S. 179, 461.

to create the rules. Just because UNLV adopted the NCAA's recruitment and eligibility rules did not transform the NCAA into a state actor.

The Court compared UNLV's adoption of NCAA rules to a state adopting the American Bar Association's (publisher of this book) ethical guidelines: It said in that situation, the ABA isn't acting for the state. The state is choosing to adopt those guidelines.

Second, the Court noted that UNLV did not delegate any power to the NCAA to take action against individual employees. UNLV's commitment to adhere to NCAA enforcement procedures was enforceable only by sanctions that the NCAA might impose on UNLV itself and not on individual employees.

Third, the Court found it significant that UNLV and the NCAA acted like adversaries in the proceedings. UNLV opposed firing its popular coach and supported him at NCAA hearings. The Court determined that the NCAA could not have been acting as an agent of UNLV from across the court. The NCAA acted more as an agent of other member schools, which compete against UNLV.

Fourth, the Court determined that the NCAA had no governmental powers when it conducted its investigation. It had no power to subpoena witnesses or to impose sanctions, and had no other authority over witnesses. Moreover, it could not directly discipline Tarkanian. Its only—and its greatest—authority was to sanction UNLV.

Fifth, the Court said that UNLV did not need to comply with the NCAA. It could have retained Tarkanian and risked sanctions, such as expulsion from the NCAA, or it could have withdrawn from the NCAA and established its own standards.

Thus, the U.S. Supreme Court reversed the Nevada Supreme Court's finding that the NCAA was a state actor when it required

UNLV to show cause why it shouldn't impose more sanctions if UNLV failed to suspend Tarkanian. The Court held that the NCAA is not a state actor.

UNLV, on the other hand, is a state actor and the Nevada Supreme Court wouldn't let UNLV fire Tarkanian.

The year after the Supreme Court's decision, Tarkanian coached UNLV to a 103–73 victory over the Duke Blue Devils to win the 1990 NCAA Men's Basketball Championship.

However, the NCAA banned post-season play for two years after the 1990 win based on the NCAA infractions from the '70s. The NCAA agreed, however, to allow UNLV to at least defend its title. The Rebels lost the 1991 NCAA Men's Basketball Championship to a Grant Hill-led Blue Devils team.

Tarkanian left UNLV in 1992 amid additional controversy. Soon after he left, he sued the NCAA for wrongfully attempting to force him out of college coaching.[3] The parties settled without an admission of liability from either side and with the NCAA paying him $2.5 million.[4] He finished his career at Fresno State in 2002.

The question of whether the NCAA could be a state actor was again raised in connection with a college basketball coach in 2007.

In 1999, Timothy Cohane, the head coach of SUNY Buffalo's men's basketball team since 1993, signed a contract extension that secured his position through April 2002.

But that didn't happen. Buffalo forced Cohane to resign in December 1999, amid an NCAA investigation. Among the viola-

---

3. *Nat'l Collegiate Athletic Ass'n v. Tarkanian*, 113 Nev. 610, 939 P.2d 1049 (Nev. Sup. Ct. 1997).

4. Edward Wong, *Tarkanian Decides It's Time to Throw in the Towel*, New York Times, March 16, 2002. Available in http://www.nytimes.com/2002/03/16/sports/college-basketball-tarkanian-decides-it-s-time-to-throw-in-the-towel.html?ref=jerry tarkanian (last visited Sept. 6, 2012).

tions alleged were that Cohane observed potential recruits play pickup basketball in the university gym.[5]

After his resignation, Buffalo officials and representatives of the NCAA continued to investigate past infractions by Cohane. Cohane later alleged that in the spring of 2000, the NCAA enforcement staff requested interviews with the student-athletes to discuss Cohane. When the student-athletes refused to interview, SUNY officials threatened that if they did not comply with the NCAA's request, the issuance of their degrees would be at risk.

The following February, at a hearing conducted by the NCAA Committee on Infractions, Cohane argued that the NCAA acted in conjunction with SUNY officials to introduce such tainted and false evidence against him.

In a written press and Internet report dated March 21, 2001, (Infractions Report) the NCAA stated that Cohane's actions were "evasive, deceptive and not credible" and "contrary to the principles of ethical conduct." It found him guilty of NCAA violations.

Based on these findings, the NCAA sanctioned Cohane by prohibiting him from coaching at any NCAA school in the future.

Without a job or prospects for a new one, Cohane filed suit against the NCAA in the U.S. District Court for the Western District of New York. He claimed that the NCAA violated his constitutional right to due process by conducting a faulty investigation, by firing him, and by publishing a "stigmatizing" report that questioned his "ethical conduct." He also claimed that the NCAA tortiously interfered with his contractual relationship with SUNY, since he had a contract through 2002 and was forced to leave in 1999.

---

5. *Cohane v. NCAA*, No. 04-cv-181S, 2005 WL 2373474 (W.D.N.Y. Sept. 27, 2005). *See also* Joe Nocera, *Standing Up to the N.C.A.A.*, New York Times, March 24, 2012, at A19.

Not surprisingly, the NCAA filed a motion to dismiss the claims. Citing the Supreme Court's *Tarkanian* decision, the district court determined that the NCAA did not engage in state action by investigating Cohane, "however unfairly," by recommending that SUNY force him to resign or by publishing the report. The court concluded that SUNY's cooperation with the NCAA's conduct did not transform its otherwise private status into state action.

On appeal to the 2d Circuit, Cohane abandoned the claim that his forced resignation deprived him of his property interest in his position as the head coach of the men's basketball team at SUNY Buffalo. Instead he argued that the Infractions Report and the university's ratification of the report's findings deprived him of his liberty interest: it defamed him and destroyed his ability to pursue his chosen occupation.

The 2d Circuit found his arguments compelling. It held: "[T]he district court erred in concluding that Cohane could prove no set of facts showing that the NCAA was a 'willful participant in joint activity with the State,' to deprive him of his liberty, to pursue his chosen occupation, without due process of law."

The panel explained the differences with the *Tarkanian* case. First, the facts relied on by the Supreme Court in *Tarkanian* were determined by a Nevada state court following a two-week bench trial. Here, by contrast, because the district court was ruling on summary judgment, the district court had to accept the allegations from the non-moving party as true, so was required to take Cohane's complaint at face value. This included allegations of collusion between the NCAA and the university, which was not present in *Tarkanian* (recall there, the NCAA and UNLV were more like adversaries).

Second, the 2d Circuit said that the allegations that Buffalo

To the Hoop 5

The Stigma-plus Test

Overturned on other grounds, the Nevada Supreme Court provided an explanation of how a plaintiff shows a violation of a liberty interest which is at the heart of Cohane's case. "[A] plaintiff must show that a 'right or status previously recognized by state law was distinctly altered or extinguished' and that his reputation was injured as a result. This test has become known as the 'stigma-plus' test, the stigma being an injury to reputation, the plus being a change in a previously recognized status." The Nevada Supreme Court recognized that the stigma associated with the dismissal from employment on grounds involving immorality or dishonesty satisfies the stigma prong of the stigma-plus test since it affects a plaintiff's ability to obtain future employment. (*Tarkanian v. NCAA*, 103 Nev. 331, 338, 339, Aug. 27, 1987.)

abused its authority to confer or withhold degrees and improperly pressured students to provide false testimony further distinguished this case from *Tarkanian*, where "there [was] no suggestion of any impropriety respecting the agreement between the NCAA and UNLV."

Third, the 2d Circuit noted that, in *Tarkanian*, the Supreme Court found that "[t]he NCAA enjoyed no governmental powers to facilitate its investigation," including the power to subpoena witnesses. In Cohane's situation, he specifically alleged that Buffalo used its authority to compel witnesses to testify against him, just as if they had been compelled by subpoena. The court observed that Cohane could show that without the state's assistance and the exercise of its coercive authority upon the student witnesses, the NCAA could not have issued the defamatory report and imposed sanctions on Cohane.

If these allegations were proven, they could show that Buffalo willfully participated in joint activity with the NCAA to deprive Cohane of his liberty.

The court noted that, while the NCAA may be able to rebut these claims and prove it did not engage in concerted action with Buffalo, the district court erred in reading *Tarkanian* to say that the NCAA can never be a state actor when it conducts an investigation of a state school. The NCAA's subsequent petition for cert was denied.

Five years later, the *Cohane* case is in the discovery stages and the Rebels are still runnin'.

Chapter 6

Flagrant Fouls:
What Standard Determines Fault when a Player Gets Hurt?

Dotzler v. Tuttle, 234 Neb. 176,
449 N.W.2d 774 (Neb. 1990)

On December 28, 1984, brothers Joseph and Ron Dotzler were playing on opposite teams during a lunch-hour pick-up game at the Omaha Southwest YMCA. On one play, Joseph went flying. It wasn't a safe landing: he fractured both his wrists.

Ron later testified that he saw Joseph standing at "about" the free throw line after making a shot at the basket when Bruce Tuttle ran at Joseph with outstretched arms, and pushed him. Ron also recalled in his testimony that when he approached Bruce after the incident, Bruce said that Joseph had been pushing him the whole game and he was "getting sick and tired of it."

Bruce remembered the incident differently. He described coming down the court on a fast break, trying to get open for a pass, not particularly aware of Joseph's presence—that the two of them "banged together," but not that he pushed Joseph, nor that he told Ron that he was tired of being pushed around by Joseph.

If it had been a friendly game, it wasn't after that. Joseph sued Bruce for both negligence and recklessness under Nebraska state law. The trial court dismissed Joseph's negligence claim but sent his recklessness claim to the jury. The jury failed to find that Bruce was reckless and Joseph appealed to the Nebraska Supreme Court.

On appeal to the Nebraska Supreme Court, Joseph argued that:

(1) his negligence claim should not have been tossed out,

(2) the judge failed to correctly define recklessness for the jury,

(3) his expert witness on the rules of a recreational basketball game should have been allowed to testify, and

(4) his possible contributory negligence should not have been posited as a question for the jury.

The court held that the question of whether Joseph's negligence claim should have gone to the jury depended on whether the participants were involved in a contact sport. And, as basketball is a contact sport, negligence does not apply—players agree to some sort of physical contacts that are foreseeable within the game. Accordingly, to impose wide tort liability, such as negligence, on sports participants could "chill the vigor of athletic competitions."

That is not to say that contact sports are an every-man-for-himself free-for-all, like the cafeteria food fight at Faber College in 1978. The court cautioned that some restraints must accompany every player on the playing field.

Accordingly, the court held that a participant in a game involving a contact sport such as basketball is liable for injuries in a tort action only if his or her conduct is either willful or done with a reckless disregard for the safety of the other player, but is not liable for ordinary negligence.

Joseph argued that the trial court's jury instruction defining recklessness was misleading because it included the word "intent." He asserted that inclusion of the word "intent" in the description of the recklessness standard, misled the jury into believing that he had to prove that Bruce acted with actual intent.

The jury instruction read, in part:

> Recklessness also differs [from negligence] in that it consists of intentionally doing an act with knowledge not only that it contains a risk of harm to others as does negligence, but that it actually involves a risk substantially greater in magnitude than is necessary in the case of negligence.

The Nebraska Supreme Court found it was Joseph who was misled on the definition of reckless: "It appears to be plaintiff's position that acting intentionally is not an element of recklessness. That is not correct."

The court held that it was the correct instruction because recklessness does include an element of intent—intent to do the act, with knowledge that it may cause harm.

So far, Joseph was 0–2 on his appeal. He also contended that the rejection of his expert witness was cause for a new trial. He wanted to offer testimony from a veteran recreational basketball player, who had played in 15,000 to 20,000 pickup games, that the way Bruce was running—too fast and without looking where he was going or caring where the other participants were located—showed a reckless disregard for the other players in the game.

The court said that the trial court was correct in not allowing the testimony—that the rules of the games that the veteran played could have been different from the recreational game Joseph and Bruce were playing that particular day. The gist of the court's ruling was that the jury was perfectly capable of

To the Hoop 6

Safety in Sports

Generally, mere negligence will not lead to a successful claim by one contact sports participant to another. The Nebraska Supreme Court looked to how other jurisdictions handled similar claims in football, hockey, soccer, and softball cases. It found that the majority of jurisdictions held that a suit by an injured participant, if not based on intentional infliction of injury, must be based on reckless disregard of safety, that an allegation of negligence is not sufficient to state a cause of action. *See Gauvin v. Clark*, 537 N.E.2d 94 (1989) (hockey); *Hackbart v. Cincinnati Bengals, Inc.*, 601 F.2d 516 (10th Cir. 1979) (football); *Nabozny v. Barnhill*, 31 Ill. App. 3d 212 (1975) (soccer); and *Ross v. Clouser*, 637 S.W.2d 11 (Mo. 1982) (softball).

determining whether Bruce acted with a reckless disregard for the safety of Joseph, without hearing the opinion of a recreational basketball player.

Finally, Joseph got a fast break. Bruce, in his answer to Joseph's initial claims, alleged that Joseph was guilty of contributory negligence, "more than slight,"[1] in failing to keep a proper lookout and by failing to control his body to avoid an impact with Bruce. The trial judge had allowed the jury to hear that defense to Joseph's claims.

The Nebraska Supreme Court, however, said that even if

---

1. *See* Nebraska Revised Statute 25-21, 185. Injuries to person or property; contributory negligence; comparative negligence. The word "slight" was probably used in the answer because in actions in Nebraska accruing before February 8, 1992, (in which this case took place) the fact that a plaintiff may have been guilty of contributory negligence did not bar recovery when the contributory negligence was "slight." So Bruce probably argued "more than slight" to preclude any recovery if negligence was found.

contributory negligence could be a defense to recklessness, the plaintiff's conduct was not at issue.

Based on the wrongful inclusion of contributory negligence, the case was remanded for a new trial. The second trial again resulted in a verdict for Bruce. Joseph didn't appeal from the second trial.

Chapter 7

Only 24 Seconds to Shoot:
The NBA and Television

Chicago Professional Sports Ltd. and WGN v. NBA,
961 F.2d 667 (7th Cir. 1992) (Bulls I); Chicago
Professional Sports Ltd. and WGN v. NBA,
95 F.3d 593 (7th Cir. 1996) (Bulls II)

You could say that in the '90s, the Chicago Bulls were the most exciting team in the NBA. As Michael Jordan ascended, the Bulls were happy to oblige their growing national fan base by broadcasting their local games across the country. They were able to do this because they were one of three NBA teams with access to a superstation, a local channel that had the capacity to broadcast nationally. At the time, the NBA allowed them to air twenty-five games on the superstation, and the Bulls took full advantage of the allotment. They signed a contract with WGN superstation that went through the 1993–1994 season.

But the NBA was growing concerned with the Bulls' infatuation with their superstation. For one, since the superstation broadcasts were shown in the markets of other NBA teams, weaker teams in smaller markets could suffer revenue losses from having to compete against the superstation telecasts. Fans wanted to watch the domination that was Michael Jordan and Scottie Pippen instead of supporting their local teams. The NBA feared this would lead to reduced local ticket sales and reduced local television rights fees for the weaker teams.[1] Weak teams don't a strong league make.

The league also needed to protect the integrity of its national broadcasts for the good of all the NBA teams. The national revenues from the NBA's TV deals were shared equally among all teams, while the Bulls received 100 percent of the revenues from WGN. The values of these national contracts could be reduced when the games selected for national broadcast were competing with the superstation broadcasts. What was the NBA to do?

The NBA Board of Governors voted to create a new league rule that would reduce the number of games individual teams could license to superstations from twenty-five to twenty.

Since the Bulls had already licensed twenty-five games to WGN, they had two options: (1) only license twenty games to WGN and forego the revenue of the additional five games, or (2) sue the NBA for the right to air the games. They chose the second option and went to court to fight for their right to air more games nationally.

The Bulls sued the NBA in the U.S. District Court for the Northern District of Illinois. They sought an injunction against the implementation of the new reduction rule, claiming that it violated Section 1 of the Sherman Act.

(As previously discussed, Section 1 of the Sherman Act prohibits agreements, combinations, or conspiracies that illegally restrain trade. Chapter Three looked at the Sherman Act in the context of franchise ownership; Chapter Four examined it in the context of a franchise relocation; this chapter will examine it within the context of limiting team broadcast rights; Chapter Ten will consider the Sherman Act with regard to player

---

1. *Chicago Professional Sports Ltd. and WGN v. NBA*, 754 F. Supp. 1336 (N.D. Ill. 1991).

restraints and the nonstatutory labor exemption; and Chapter Fourteen will discuss its application to student-athletes.)

The Bulls alleged that the league's decision to reduce the number of superstation games a team could air constituted an agreement among the other NBA teams to restrain trade by reducing output. The reduction in output injured both the team and the station by impeding a source of revenue as well as non-monetary injuries: less exposure and fewer opportunities to build a strong and permanent following for the Bulls; lost opportunity for WGN to run on-air promotions for the rest of its programming during the Bulls telecasts.[2]

In response, the NBA implemented a triangle defense. It argued that:

(1) the limitation was insulated from a Sherman Act violation under Section 1291 of the Sports Broadcasting Act of 1966 (SBA);

(2) even if the Sherman Act applied, the five-game reduction had no significant effect, if any, on trade; and

(3) even if the reduction rule was a restraint on trade, it was not an unreasonable restraint on trade.

Under Section 1291 of the SBA, individual professional sports teams can pool their sponsored television rights and the respective leagues may sell them to a television network as a single package without running afoul of antitrust laws.

That sounds good, but the district court determined that the SBA did not apply to the reduction rule. The SBA only exempts those telecasting rights that have been transferred or sold by the league.

Since the Bulls—and not the league—sold the TV rights to WGN, the league could not regulate or reduce those games with-

2. *Chicago Professional Sports Ltd. and WGN v. NBA, supra* at 1353 N.D. Ill. 1991.

in the SBA antitrust exemption. Therefore, the court found the SBA inapplicable and subjected the league's reduction rule to analysis under the Sherman Act.[3]

Just because the Sherman Act applies to an agreement, doesn't necessarily mean the agreement violates it. In the context of sports, courts usually apply a rule of reason analysis—they will weigh an agreement's procompetitive benefits against its anticompetitive effects in a specific market to determine whether such a violation has occurred.

So market definition and market power usually determine whether the agreement has the potential for "genuine adverse effects on competition" under the rule of reason. Such that, the smaller the market, the greater the impact on competition therein, and the larger the market, the lesser the impact.[4]

Where the adverse effects are directly observable, however, as is the case where there is a reduction in games to be broadcast, the district court determined that market power is not required to find antitrust liability under rule of reason. Instead, the court applied a "quick look" version of the rule of reason by considering whether there was a "sound" justification for the restraints.

The district court found significant restraints on trade:

    (1) the rule divides the markets and controls output;

    (2) it restricts output in the national market and in the local market;

    (3) it reduces games and exposure;

    (4) the refusal to deal with superstations is basically an agreement to stop selling to certain customers;

    (5) it reduces competition between teams and the league by ousting competition between individual teams

---

3. *Chicago Professional Sports Ltd. and WGN, supra* at 1350–52.
4. *Chicago Professional Sports Ltd. and WGN, supra.*

and the league to the extent they compete for viewers;

    (6) teams can't respond to consumer preference; and

    (7) the market was not deciding.

The court also noted a significant reduction in output—it found that the five-game reduction decreased the number of games available to viewers nationwide and shrunk the options open to advertisers for reaching those viewers.

It then looked to whether there were sound justifications for the reduction. Although the NBA proffered several reasons for imposing the reduction, the court found that none of them were acceptable and deemed the rule an illegal restraint of trade. The court enjoined the NBA from enforcing the rule under this "quick look" version of the rule of reason.

Enjoined from enforcing its rule, the NBA appealed the ruling. So the Bulls and the NBA met again. This time in the 7th Circuit. In *Bulls I* (*Chicago Professional Sports Ltd. and WGN v. NBA*, 961 F.2d 667 (7th Cir. 1992)), Judge Frank Easterbrook wrote the decision for the panel and addressed each of the NBA's arguments as to: (1) the SBA exemption, (2) application of the rule of reason, and (3) free-riding by the Bulls.

Judge Easterbrook agreed with the district court that the SBA antitrust exemption did not safeguard the NBA's rule. Under the SBA, the NBA could only regulate games it had the right to broadcast. The 7th Circuit held that the NBA could not limit the Bulls' superstation games to twenty broadcasts because the Bulls—not the NBA—actually owned the rights to forty-one broadcasts.

But the NBA had argued that was just semantics. It contended that it could have limited WGN to twenty games by merely obtaining the rights to all of the games and then relicensing only twenty games to each team.

The 7th Circuit wrote that it wasn't that simple. There was no guarantee that all of the clubs would agree to such a transfer of all of the rights in every game since such a transfer would have a major effect on the allocation of revenues among the clubs. National revenues are divided among the clubs, while each team keeps its local revenues. Accordingly, the panel said the NBA may not have received the agreement it expected.

Not wanting to leave the league in a lurch, the court hypothesized various ways the NBA could limit a team's games that would be consistent with Section 1291 of the SBA:

> The league might have put a cap of 20 superstation games in its contracts with NBC and Turner, [that way the limit is on rights the league transferred] or it might have followed the path of professional baseball and allowed unlimited broadcasting over superstations while claiming a portion of the revenues for distribution among the clubs.

The NBA had also contended that the district court failed to define a market in its rule of reason analysis and that the first step of any rule of reason analysis is to define a market to determine the effect, if any, of the purported restraint.

The court heard the NBA out regarding its definition of a market, but ultimately found such a discussion irrelevant. As the court said,

> [A]ny agreement to reduce output measured by the number of televised games requires some justification—some explanation connecting the practice to consumers' benefits—before the court attempts an analysis of market power. Unless there are sound justifications, the court condemns the practice without ado, using the "quick look" version of the Rule of Reason . . .

As to the league's argument that the cutback was only five games, the court said:

> [L]ong ago the Court rejected the invitation to inquire into the "reasonableness" of price and output decisions. E.g., *United States v. Trenton Potteries Co.*, 273 U.S. 392, 47 S. Ct. 377, 71 L. Ed. 700 (1927); *United States v. Socony–Vacuum Oil Co.*, 310 U.S. 150, 60 S. Ct. 811, 84 L. Ed. 1129 (1940). Competition in markets, not judges, sets price and output. A court applying the Rule of Reason asks whether a practice produces net benefits for consumers; it is no answer to say that a loss is "reasonably small." (What is more, if five superstation games is tiny in relation to the volume of telecasting, the benefits from the limitation are correspondingly small.)

Consequently, even though he knocked out the NBA's justifications for the limitation rule, Judge Easterbrook found the NBA's description of a free-riding problem compelling.

The NBA argued that the reduction in games was justified because the Bulls were free-riding on the NBA's coattails.

First, the league's contracts with NBC and TNT required those networks to advertise NBA basketball during their other programs, giving the Bulls and WGN the benefit of the promotion of basketball without paying the cost of those advertisements.

Second, the NBA has revenue-sharing devices and the draft to help the weaker teams. The Bulls took full advantage of these when they were weak (in 1984, they received the third pick in the draft and drafted Michael Jordan). The Bulls now want to keep the revenue from the national telecasts for themselves.

Third, the Bulls took advantage of the other cooperative

efforts of the members of the league that helped build basket-ball as a rival to football and baseball.

Judge Easterbrook ultimately wrote that although control of free riding is an accepted justification for cooperation, it is not a justification for reducing output. Basically, you can control free riding without turning it into an antitrust issue. He questioned why the NBA couldn't just levy a charge for each game on the superstation or have the Bulls surrender a portion of revenues. (Recall, in Chapter Four, that the NFL charged the Raiders for the usurpation of a franchise opportunity, as the NBA later did to the Clippers).

In his opinion, Judge Easterbrook also briefly noted that parts of the NBA's position "verge on the argument that a sports league is a single entity as a matter of law." (Single Entity Status would exempt the NBA from application of Section 1 of the Sherman Act since Section 1 requires an "agreement" to restrain trade. A single entity cannot agree with itself.) He didn't, however, discuss that possibility further. He said that since the NBA did not contend in the district court that the NBA is a single entity, and barely did so on appeal, it was not ripe for review. He did provide some foresight:

> Whether a sports league is a single entity for anti-trust purposes has significance far beyond this case, and it would be imprudent to decide the question after such cursory dialog. Perhaps the parties will join issue more fully in the proceedings still to come in the district court. For now we treat the NBA as a joint venture, just as the parties do in the bulk of their arguments.

With that, the 7th Circuit affirmed the district court's finding that the NBA violated the Sherman Act with its reduction rule, and also left the NBA with some ideas on how to overcome the free-riding problem and comply with the SBA.

After losing its appeal, the NBA, in another attempt to restrict the Bulls' superstation programming, added a provision in its *contract with TNT* that prohibited all NBA teams from televising their games on a superstation on the same night that TNT was airing a national NBA game.

Nonetheless, in a new lawsuit, the Bulls fought this restriction as well. The district court again found that nothing in the NBA agreement with TNT indicated that the clubs agreed to transfer all copyrights to the network, as the SBA requires. The court said that agreeing to cap the telecasts is not the same as having the league transfer all or some of the games to the network. It is still regulating games in which it does not own any rights.

Just like their championship record in 1993 the Bulls were three for three. The NBA did not appeal the latest ruling. Instead, it rearranged its television rights structure based on a suggestion from the 7th Circuit in *Bulls I*:

(1) It amended its bylaws so that all of the teams transfer all of their copyrights in their games to the league;

(2) It then assigned to NBC exclusive rights to televise all 1,100 regular-season games;

(3) NBC kept 25–26 total games to air nationally and agreed to authorize the NBA to relicense to a superstation no more than 85 of the remaining games with no more than 15 of those 85 games to include any one team;

(4) The NBA then permitted Turner to select up to 85 of the remaining games to air on its cable network TNT and its superstation WTBS;

(5) Once Turner picked its games, the NBA could authorize individual teams to telecast remaining games on local

---

5. *Chicago Professional Sports Ltd. and WGN v. NBA*, 808 F. Supp. 646 (N.D. Ill. 1992).

channels, but not to more than 5 million television house-holds outside their home territory (this basically precluded superstation use, because there wasn't at the time, a method to cut the signal once it reached 5 million homes); and

(6) The NBA directed that if the above restriction on superstations was struck down, then a club that chose to use a superstation would have to pay a fee to the NBA.[6]

Now the Bulls were seeing red. The NBA had stripped them completely from airing any games on WGN. They filed a new suit in the district court. This time they asked for the right to air forty-one games on WGN without any additional fees.

The NBA was ready on defense.

The NBA elaborated on the single-entity theory it had alluded to in its appellate brief in *Bulls I*. It argued that the NBA is a single entity incapable of conspiring with itself. According to this theory, the Sherman Act could not apply to the NBA's actions.

To support its contention, the league relied on the U.S. Supreme Court decision in *Copperweld v. Independence Tube Corp.*, 467 U.S. 752 (1984), in which the Court held that because a corporation and its wholly owned subsidiary have a complete unity of interest, they are a single enterprise for purposes of Section 1 of the Sherman Act.

The district court found that while the NBA does have some cooperative characteristics, the NBA confused the cooperation that is beneficial in a joint venture (where two distinct parties cooperate) with the unified interest inherent in a single entity.

The court said that the NBA lacks a "complete unity of interest." It looked to the fact that the teams compete in various areas: for points on the court, players, fans, coaches, general

---

6. *Chicago Professional Sports Ltd. and WGN v. NBA*, 874 F. Supp. 844 (N.D. Ill. 1995).

managers, advertising dollars, and ticket sales. Moreover, each NBA team is separately owned and controlled. At its core, the NBA is a joint venture of at least two ventures that previously pursued their own interests.

The district court concluded that all cooperation among separately incorporated firms is forbidden under Section 1 of the Sherman Act, except where a parent corporation and its wholly owned subsidiary have a "complete unity of interest."

So after determining that the Sherman Act applied to the NBA, the court looked to whether the NBA's revised television rights structure fell under the SBA exemption to the act.

The district court agreed with the NBA, that by transferring the rights to all 1,100 games to NBC, the NBA brought itself within the purview of Section 1291 of the SBA, but the court concluded that the NBA failed to comply with Section 1292.

Section 1292 is an exception to the antitrust exemption. Whereas Section 1291 permits the pooling of television rights, Section 1292 voids the exemption if the league puts territorial restrictions on where the rights holders may air their games.

The district court noted that the NBA "purportedly" transferred the exclusive rights to televise all regular-season NBA games to NBC, but that NBC agreed to broadcast only twenty-five of them, then retransferred the remaining games back to the NBA to relicense, subject to limitations. One of those limitations was that an individual team could broadcast to no more than 5 million television households outside of their home territory.

The court thus found that the NBA limited where the Bulls may broadcast their games in violation of Section 1292 of the SBA, which prohibits such territorial restrictions.

So the SBA exemption did not apply.

To review, the court deemed the NBA a joint venture capable of conspiring and found that its television rights structure fell outside the SBA exemption. Moving on, the court found the rule clearly reduced output below the market demand, illegally restraining trade. The new rule completely wiped out WGN's ability to show any Bulls games at all and audiences wanted to see *those games*. It reasoned that the rule was basically a resolution among competitors (the teams) to divide markets (territorial limitations) and restrain output (limit the teams' superstation games).

So it again applied a "quick look" review to the restraints. U.S. District Court Judge Hubert Will shot down each one of the NBA's procompetitive justifications for its latest set of restraints, finding that the NBA produced no evidence that the elimination of WGN would be procompetitive. The substance of the structure, he said, had not changed.

Ultimately, the district court agreed that charging some fee was appropriate to combat a free-rider problem, but that the fee could not be set unreasonably high to restrict output and cause an antitrust issue. He ordered the NBA not to limit the superstation broadcasts to less than thirty superstation telecasts.[7]

To put it in perspective, during the Bulls' first three-championship run with Michael Jordan, fans throughout the country could see twenty-five Bulls games (for free) in addition to those on the NBA's national broadcast. Then, in January 1995, the district court raised that number to thirty. During this time, the Bulls paid no additional tax, fine, or fee for the extra *air* time.

That all changed after the next appeal. The Bulls appealed because they wanted to air forty-one games on WGN. The NBA appealed because its television structure was in question. Thus, it set out to show why the Sherman Act shouldn't apply at all.

On appeal, Judge Easterbrook, again speaking for the panel, addressed the NBA's single entity defense.

---

7. *Chicago Professional Sports Ltd. and WGN v. NBA*, 874 F. Supp. at 862.

He rejected the district court's opinion that all cooperation between firms, except to the extent they have a complete unity of interest, is forbidden by Section 1 because even single firms don't have a complete unity of interest.[8]

The panel read *Copperweld* to hold that like a single firm, a parent-subsidiary cooperates internally to **increase efficiency**. On the other hand, a cartel uses concerted action to "deprive[s] the marketplace of the **independent centers of decision making** that competition assumes." Entities in the **middle** of these opposites **reduce the number of independent decision-makers**, yet may still **improve efficiency**. They include: "mergers, joint ventures, and various vertical agreements" (emphasis added).

The panel noted that under this typology, "there is no reason why the NBA can't be treated as a single firm." The court then proceeded to weigh the NBA's "single entity" characteristics against its "joint venture" characteristics.

1. Single Entity Characteristics

(1) The NBA produces a single product: NBA basketball.

(2) The NBA competes with other basketball leagues (both college and professional), other sports, such as baseball and football, and other forms of entertainment, such as plays, movies, opera, TV shows, Disneyland, and Las Vegas.

2. Joint Venture Characteristics

(1) There are thirty different clubs with individual owners that have the right to secede and rearrange into two or three leagues.

(2) The NBA was assembled from clubs that formerly belonged to other leagues.

---

8. *Chicago Professional Sports Ltd. and WGN v. NBA*, 95 F.3d 593 (*Bulls II*).

To the Hoop 7

Sports Leagues and the Single Entity

In 2010, the U.S. Supreme Court, in *American Needle v. NFL*, 130 S. Ct. 2201 (2010), held that for Section 1 purposes, when it comes to the marketing of NFL teams' individually owned intellectual property, the NFL is not a single entity. The opinion appeared to be limited to the NFL's treatment of its teams' intellectual property.

In December 2012, District Court Judge Shira Scheindlin, sitting in the U.S. District Court for the Southern District of New York, extended the *American Needle* holding to include team broadcast rights. Judge Scheindlin wrote: "*American Needle* conclusively established that these kinds of arrangements are subject to Section 1 scrutiny."[1]

In *Laumann*, baseball and hockey fans had sued the MLB and the NHL. They argued that the leagues limit the live television and Internet broadcasts of baseball and hockey games in violation of the Sherman Act. The fans claimed that blackout rules and expensive out-of-market broadcast packages, restrict output, which harms competition. The leagues countered that "*American Needle* did not preclude the single-entity doctrine for all league conduct." In addition, the leagues attempted to differentiate team-owned IP at issue in *American Needle*, from league-owned and controlled out-of-market telecast rights.

This litigation is ongoing. It is not clear how the 2d Circuit would rule, if given the opportunity to do so. The 2d Circuit might very well find *American Needle* is limited to the marketing of team intellectual property, and like the 7th Circuit in *Bulls II*, not rule out the possibility that when acting in the broadcast market, a sports league could constitute a single entity for Section 1 purposes. Keep an eye out.

---

1. *Laumann v. National Hockey League*, No. 12 Civ. 1817, 2012 WL 6043225 (S.D.N.Y. Dec. 5, 2012).

The court concluded that "the league looks more or less like a firm depending on which facet of the business one examines." For example, from the fan's perspective, it is a single entity that gives them NBA basketball, but from the college basketball player's perspective, each team is a potential employer. Judge Easterbrook wrote:

> Sports are sufficiently diverse that it is essential to investigate their organization and ask *Copperweld*'s functional question one league at a time—and perhaps one facet of a league at a time, for we do not rule out the possibility that an organization such as the NBA is best understood as one firm when selling broadcast rights to a network in competition with a thousand other producers of entertainment, but is best understood as a joint venture when curtailing competition for players who have few other market opportunities.

Although Judge Easterbrook observed that, ". . . when acting in the broadcast market the NBA is closer to a single firm than to a group of independent firms," the panel ultimately held that it was not for it to decide whether the NBA is a single firm. It thus directed the district court to evaluate the question on remand and inquire into the NBA's market power.

In the meantime, Judge Easterbrook lifted the injunction and required the Bulls and WGN to respect the league's limitations on the maximum number of superstation telecasts.

The parties settled and the case was never heard on remand.[9] Thus, a determination of whether the NBA is a single entity (at least for broadcasting purposes) was never ultimately decided.

---

9. Reuters Limited, Dec. 12, 1996, *Tribune's WGN-TV, Chicago Bulls Settle Suit with NBA.*

Chapter 8

Keeping Trax of Steals per Game:

Can a Basketball Game Be Copyrighted?

NBA v. Motorola, Inc., 939 F. Supp. 1071
(S.D.N.Y. 1996), *rev'd*, 105 F.3d 841 (2d Cir. 1997)

In 1996, before smart phones and tweets ruled the world, Motorola manufactured and sold the SportsTrax pager device, which reported instantaneous information about professional basketball games to its customers.

Motorola contracted with Sports Team Analysis and Tracking Systems, Inc. d/b/a Stats, Inc., to collect information, which Motorola would then resell to the public via the SportsTrax pager. Stats' employees would watch NBA games on TV or listen to them on the radio and contemporaneously key in the live game statistics to a computer that would then transmit the information to personal pagers and a website. Consumers could buy the SportsTrax device for $200 a pop.

The NBA was bothered by what appeared to be the copying or stealing of its real-time game information. It wanted to put an end to the practice. So it sued to enjoin Motorola and Stats (collectively referred to here as just "Motorola") from disseminating its valuable information.

The NBA claimed it owned the real-time game information and that Motorola's use and distribution of it constituted, *inter alia*, copyright infringement and commercial misappropriation. Therefore, it thought it could stop them.

To establish copyright infringement, the NBA needed to prove: (1) it owned a valid copyright; and (2) Motorola copied the original elements in its copyrighted work.

The district court for the Southern District of New York began its decision by determining whether the NBA had a valid copyright in the information derived from a game or in the game itself. It tackled this by first defining a copyright—it is an original work of authorship that is fixed in a tangible medium.

The court then examined whether a copyright's requirements of originality, authorship, and fixation applied to game facts and live sporting events.

Originality is comprised of two components: (1) the work must be created independently, as opposed to being copied from another work; and (2) the work must possess some minimal degree of creativity.

Facts are not protectable because they lack the requisite originality. The court noted that "[t]he first person to find and report a particular fact has not created the fact; he or she has merely discovered its existence." The court noted that ideas, although they may possess some degree of originality, are not protectable because they are not expressions of originality.

This is referred to as the idea/expression dichotomy. The court observed that "Congress wanted to reward an individual's ingenuity and effort while at the same time permitting others to benefit from improvements on the same subject matter. Therefore, you can't protect a mere fact or idea, but you can protect the original expression of that idea." The district court concluded that facts from a game do not have the requisite originality.

Moving on, the court recognized that it would be challenging to determine the "author" of a game, because there are the "referees, coaches, and . . . other participants whose creative energies contributed to the NBA game."

It further noted that live sporting events are noticeably absent from the list of works of authorship identified in the Copyright Act. The Copyright Act explicitly lists eight categories of works of authorship that include:

(1) literary works;

(2) musical works, including any accompanying words;

(3) dramatic works, including any accompanying music;

(4) pantomimes and choreographic works;

(5) pictorial, graphic, and sculptural works;

(6) motion pictures and other audiovisual works;

(7) sound recordings; and

(8) architectural works. (17 U.S.C. Section 102(a).)

Although the list is merely illustrative, the court noted that in amending the Copyright Act, Congress actually contemplated and then rejected giving copyright protection to sporting events. In other words, a live basketball game lacks the authorship requirement necessary for copyright protection.

Lastly, the court examined the fixation requirement. Parsing the legislative history of the 1976 amendment to the Copyright Act, the court emphasized Congress's intent to make the simultaneous broadcast of a game meet the fixation requirement, but not the underlying event:

> [T]he bill seeks to resolve, through the definition of "fixation" in section 101, the status of live broadcasts— sports, news coverage, live performances of music, etc.—that are reaching the public in unfixed form but that are simultaneously being recorded. When a football game is being covered by four television cameras, with

a director guiding the activities of the four cameramen and choosing which of their electronic images are sent out to the public and in what order, there is little doubt that what the cameramen and the director are doing constitutes "authorship." The further question to be considered is whether there has been a fixation. If the images and sounds to be broadcast are first recorded (on a video tape, film, etc.) and then are transmitted, the recorded work would be considered a "motion picture" subject to statutory protection against unauthorized reproduction. If the program content is transmitted live to the public while being recorded at the same time, the case would be treated the same; the copyright owner would not be forced to rely on common law rather than statutory rights in proceeding against an infringing user of the live broadcast.

The district court concluded that a live NBA game does not receive copyright protection. The broadcast of the same game, however, does.

And, the court found that Motorola did not infringe on that broadcast of the game. It held that the NBA failed to satisfy the second element of a copyright infringement claim, that the defendants copied the "'constituent elements of the [broadcast] that are original.'"

The only elements that Motorola copied were the purely factual information encompassed in the score, time remaining, team with possession, quarter, and field goals per player, not the original features that render broadcasts protectable, such as those that constitute the original authorship (for example, camera angles). The court said that a "defendant is not liable for infringing a copyright if the defendant copied only unprotectable elements of the copyrighted work."

So, district court dismissed the NBA's claim of copyright infringement.

Although the district court found no copyright infringement, it nonetheless enjoined Motorola from using the game-time information under a misappropriation theory. (The court actually dismissed all of the causes of action except for the misappropriation of the games themselves.) In finding that Motorola misappropriated the game-time information, the court discussed the (1) copyright preemption doctrine and (2) New York's misappropriation cause of action.

The preemption doctrine abolishes any claims brought under state law that are equivalent to those embodied in the Copyright Act. There are two criteria, both of which must be met, to preempt a state law claim. They are (1) the general scope requirement and (2) the subject matter requirement.

A state law claim meets the general scope requirement if it seeks to vindicate any of the exclusive rights set forth in Section 106 of the Copyright Act.

> . . . [T]he owner of the copyright under this title has the exclusive rights to do and to authorize any of the following: (1) to reproduce the copyrighted work in copies or phonorecords; (2) to prepare derivative works based upon the copyrighted work; (3) to distribute copies or phonorecords of the copyrighted work to the public by sale or other transfer of ownership, or by rental, lease, or lending; (4) in the case of literary, musical, dramatic, and choreographic works, pantomimes, and motion pictures and other audiovisual works, to perform the copyrighted work publicly; (5) in the case of literary, musical, dramatic, and choreographic works, pantomimes, and pictorial, graphic, or sculptural works, including the individual images of a motion picture or other audiovisual work,

to display the copyrighted work publicly; and (6) in the case of sound recordings, to perform the copyrighted work publicly by means of a digital audio transmission.[1]

However, if there is an "extra element" required to complete the violation of a state claim—such as a claim based upon a breach of confidentiality (because that might include a breach of contract and reproduction of information)—then the claim would fall outside the general scope requirement.

The district court wrote that because the NBA's claims sought to vindicate Section 106 rights, such as distribution and reproduction of game information, the NBA's misappropriation claim failed to include an "the extra element," leaving it indistinguishable from a copyright claim. Thus, the general scope requirement of preemption was met.

However, as both the general scope and subject matter requirements must be met for preemption of a claim, the district court next looked to see if the claim fell within the subject matter requirement.

A state law claim meets the subject matter requirement if the state law protects the same type of work that falls within the "subject matter" of Sections 102 or 103 of the Copyright Act. For example, since the Copyright Act protects the simultaneous broadcast of NBA games, a misappropriation claim as to those broadcasts would be preempted.

But since the Copyright Act does not protect the game itself (as discussed above), is the copying of game information from the games preempted? Does it matter if the factual information was copied from the uncopyrightable underlying game (someone sitting in the arena) or the copyrightable simultaneous broadcast (watching on TV)?

---

1. 17 U.S.C. § 106.

Motorola did not copy elements from the underlying game. The Stats folks were not in the arena. Instead, they were watching them on TV. Thus, Motorola copied elements from the copyrightable broadcast.

So, since the game information came from the broadcast, which is subject to copyright protection, is a claim as to the misappropriation of that game information preempted? Or, can the claim proceed since the facts from the game or its broadcast are not subject to copyright protection in the first place?

To resolve this confusion, the district court created a partial preemption doctrine to fit the situation.

> [I]t is difficult to conceive of a scenario when misappropriation of rights in the broadcast (which is preempted) does not also involve misappropriation of rights in the underlying event (which is not preempted). After all, the skill, expenditures, and labor involved in the broadcast would seem to constitute nothing more than an inseparable supplement to the skill, expenditure, and labor involved in the game itself, for the broadcast would not exist but for the skill, expenditure, and labor used to create the game. Thus, misappropriation of one subsumes misappropriation of the other, yet only that part relating to the broadcast would be preempted.[2]

The court explained that if you take elements from one, you are by definition taking elements from the other, but noted that only elements from the broadcast are actually preempted. This leads to two claims for what is basically the same work: (1) copyright infringement of a broadcast, and (2) misappropriation of the underlying event.

---

2. 937 F. Supp. at 1167 n. 22.

To avoid this bifurcation of a single event, the court felt it would be required to hold that NBA games, as opposed to just their telecasts, fall within the subject matter of copyright protection, which would "result in total preemption of a misappropriation claim."

It thought total preemption was inappropriate, and chose not to interpret the Copyright Act as sanctioning such a harsh result. Instead, the district court held that the information taken from an NBA game, whether from the telecast or live, can be subject to a misappropriation claim.

Having found that the copying of the game-time information was not preempted, the district court looked to whether Motorola misappropriated it.

The district court wrote that there is no specific list in New York of what constitutes misappropriation, just that the law of unfair competition in New York is a broad and flexible doctrine. The court thus held that by depriving the NBA "of the just benefits of its labors and expenditures in respect of the creation and production of [NBA] games and public dissemination of descriptions and accounts thereof," Motorola commercially misappropriated the NBA's proprietary rights in the NBA games in violation of New York common law.

The district court granted a permanent injunction against Motorola's continued sale of the pager.

Motorola appealed the injunction to the 2d Circuit, contending that the district court erred in its finding of a partial preemption and therefore the misappropriation claim should be tossed out entirely.

Although the NBA did not appeal its adverse copyright infringement decision, the 2d Circuit reiterated the principles of copyright protection to set up its preemption decision.

It started its decision by reiterating that only (a) original works of authorship that are (b) fixed in a tangible medium, receive copyright protection.

First, like the district court, it held the underlying game does not constitute a work of authorship, as does the filmed event. Because there are so many "players" involved, it would be challenging to determine a single author. In addition, preparation for a game is more of a hope as to how it will turn out rather than an authored determination of what will actually happen. So, like the district court, the 2d Circuit found there is no author.

Second, the court held the Copyright Act was amended in 1976 to specifically include simultaneously recorded transmissions of live performances and sporting events in the definition of "fixation." The definition, however, was not amended to include the underlying works themselves, again in accordance with the district court.

Because the underlying game was not subject to copyright protection and Motorola did not copy the broadcast of the game, there was no copyright infringement.

The 2d Circuit also agreed with the district court that facts of the game are not subject to copyright protection. Since Motorola only reproduced the facts from the broadcasts, not the expression or description of the game used in the broadcast, it did not infringe the NBA's copyright in the broadcast.

That's where their similarities ended.

The 2d Circuit found no basis for a partial preemption doctrine. Reversing the district court's finding, it examined the interplay of preemption and misappropriation, unlike the district court, which examined them separately.

As you recall from the discussion above, the subject matter requirement refers to a right that the Copyright Act protects (books, movies, paintings, and so on).

The district court summed up the situation as follows:

where game information is taken from a non-copyrightable work (in this case, a live NBA game), it does not fall within the subject matter of copyright. But, where the game information is taken from the copyrightable work (the broadcast of the game), it falls within the subject matter of copyright.

Under the district court's partial preemption doctrine, however, where the same game information can be obtained from either source, it should be deemed as falling outside the subject matter, regardless from which source it derives.

The 2d Circuit found the opposite to be true: Where the same facts can be taken from non-copyrightable or copyrightable work, it said that the facts fall within the subject matter of copyright. Game information, the 2d Circuit held, meets the subject matter requirement for preemption.

Copyrightable material often contains uncopyrightable elements within it, but copyright preemption bars state law misappropriation claims with respect to the uncopyrightable as well as the copyrightable elements. The court rejected the possibility of a partial preemption doctrine where a single game could provide two causes of action: (1) copyright infringement, in the broadcast of the game, and (2) misappropriation of the facts in the underlying event or game.

Moving on, the 2d Circuit explained how the misappropriation claim could still avoid preemption if it falls outside the general scope requirement by containing an extra element.

On this point, the 2d Circuit looked to the "extra element" test we addressed earlier.

Recall that the general scope requirement is met where the state law claim seeks to vindicate rights equivalent to copyright, such as through reproduction, performance, distribution, or display. If an additional element is required in the state law claim, the claim would fall outside the general scope and avoid preemption.

An extra element must be significant. It cannot be mere "intent." The 2d Circuit determined that a "hot news" claim, as defined by the U.S. Supreme Court in *International News Service v. Associated Press*, 248 U.S. 215, would suffice as meeting the extra element exception to preemption. (INS would take factual stories from East Coast AP papers and wire them to INS papers on the West Coast that had yet to publish because of time difference.)

Under *INS*, a defendant's copying of facts at the precise point when the facts are of highest commercial value, with no expense to the defendant, constitutes unlawful misappropriation.

The 2d Circuit identified the extra elements to copyright infringement that allow a "hot news" claim to survive preemption as:

(1) the time-sensitive value of factual information,

(2) the threat to the very existence of the product or service provided by the plaintiff, and

(3) the free riding by a defendant.

Applying these factors, the court held that Motorola's use did not constitute "hot news" misappropriation.

First, it conceded that the collection and retransmission of strictly factual information about the games (box scores in newspapers, summaries of statistics on television sports news, and real-time facts to be transmitted to pagers) that Motorola used was in fact time-sensitive.

As to the second factor, the court did not believe that Motorola used the information to compete with the NBA's main products.

With regard to the NBA's primary products—producing basketball games with live attendance and

93

To the Hoop 8

Protecting the Game

Motorola teaches us that a live basketball game is not subject to copyright protection, but its simultaneous broadcast is. That is not to say that one can freely take pictures and videos from inside an arena without consequence. Tickets to events serve as the contracts, and by entering the arena, attendees bind themselves to the terms. Ticket backs usually contain a provision to the following effect: No recording or transmission of any description, account, picture, or reproduction of event permitted.

For more on the binding nature of sporting event ticket-back language, *see Morris v. PGA, 364 F.3d 1288* (11th Cir. 2004) (finding that the PGA may prohibit the unauthorized public dissemination or commercial usage of its compilation of real-time golf scores by contract); *Bicket v. Buffalo Bills, Inc.*, 472 N.Y.S.2d 245 (1983) (finding the ticket-back language enforceable as to the revocability of the ticket); and *Ganey v. New York Jets Football Club*, 550 N.Y.S.2d 566 (N.Y. City Civ. Ct. 1990) (holding the terms on the ticket back: "Tickets cannot be replaced if lost, stolen or destroyed" binding).

licensing copyrighted broadcasts of those games—there is no evidence that anyone regards SportsTrax or the AOL site as a substitute for attending NBA games or watching them on television. In fact, Motorola markets SportsTrax as being designed "for those times when you cannot be at the arena, watch the game on TV, or listen to the radio . . ."[3]

Third, the 2d Circuit determined that an indispensable element of an *INS* "hot-news" claim is free riding by a defendant

---

3. *NBA v. Motorola, Inc.*, 105 F.3d 841, 854.

on a plaintiff's product. It found that Motorola did not free-ride off the NBA in its use of the SportsTrax device. Motorola had employed its own reporters to watch games and input the information.

Accordingly, the 2d Circuit vacated the injunction and dismissed the NBA's misappropriation claim.

Four months after winning the lawsuit, Motorola stopped promoting the SportsTrax device. Instead, it began promoting a new product it developed with ESPN, called "ESPN to Go," which also offered news and scores from various sports as well as pager service.[4] Today, there is likely an app for that.

---

4. *See* http://www.nytimes.com/1997/06/02/business/motorola-sidelines-device-providing-live-nba-scores.html (last visited Sept. 14, 2012).

Chapter 9

Off the Court and into the Stands:

NBA Commissioner's Authority

NBA v. NBPA, No. 04 Civ. 9528GBD,
2005 WL 22869, not reported in F. Supp. 2d,
176 L.R.R.M. (BNA) 2487 (S.D.N.Y. 2005)

O n November 19, 2004, the Indiana Pacers were leading the Detroit Pistons 97–82, with 45.9 seconds left to go, when the Pacers' Ron Artest (now Metta World Peace[1]) fouled Detroit's Ben Wallace during his basket attempt. Immediately following the foul, Wallace turned and shoved Artest in the chin. A melee ensued. Artest's and Wallace's teammates jumped into the ruckus and it was difficult to tell whether they were attempting to protect their comrades or throwing some punches of their own.

Artest made his way to the scorer's table and stretched out under the protective guard of a coach's arms. However, bulky biceps couldn't protect him from a questionable substance that one fan dumped on him.

Sideline reporter Jim Gray, who was next to Artest at the scorer's table described his take of the situation to ESPN: "A

---

1. *See* http://espn.go.com/los-angeles/nba/story/_/id/6977866/los-angeles-lakers-ron-artest-name-now-officially-metta-world-peace (last visited Sept. 5, 2012).

fan came and threw a beer and a bottle on him from point blank range.[2] When he got hit by that, he erupted . . ."[3]

Artest responded by entering the stands and attacking his presumed aggressor.[4] Artest's teammates Stephen Jackson and Anthony Johnson followed him into the stands while an arena usher restrained fellow Pacer Jermaine O'Neal. O'Neal shoved the usher and then struck a spectator.[5] Fans and players alike exchanged punches amid flying bottles, liquid, and other debris.

The game was called and a shell-shocked Pistons coach Larry Brown announced through the sound system for everyone to leave.

The next day NBA Commissioner David Stern suspended indefinitely all of the players who participated in the altercation pending further investigation. The day after that, Commissioner Stern announced specific suspensions: Artest for the rest of the season, O'Neal for twenty-five games, Johnson for five games, and Jackson for thirty games.

In issuing the suspensions, the NBA distributed a letter to each suspended player citing Section 35(d) of the NBA Constitution as authority for his suspension. Section 35(d) states:

> If in the opinion of the Commissioner any other act or conduct of a Player ***at or during an Exhibition, Regular Season or Playoff game*** [emphasis added] has been prejudicial to or against the best interests of the Association or the game of basketball, the Commis-

---

2. The fan was Jon Green. He recalled tossing Diet Coke on Artest. *See* ESPN.com news services (November 2009). *See* http://sports.espn.go.com/nba/news/story?id=4670842 (last visited Sept. 5, 2012).

3. ESPN coverage of the event. Reviewed on YouTube at 5:41.

4. *See* ESPN.com news services (November 2009). *See* http://sports.espn.go.com/nba/news/story?id=4670842 (last visited Sept. 5, 2012). (Green recalled seeing Artest grab the wrong person.)

5. *NBA v. NBPA*, No. 04 Civ. 9528GBD, 2005 WL 22869, not reported in F. Supp. 2d, 176 L.R.R.M. (BNA) 2487 (S.D.N.Y. Jan. 3, 2005).

sioner shall impose upon such Player a fine not exceeding $35,000, or may order for a time the suspension of any such Player from any connection or duties with Exhibition, Regular Season or Playoff games or he may order both such fine and suspension.

The players were not thrilled with the suspensions. So, on their behalf, the union (the NBPA) appealed the suspensions to a third-party grievance arbitrator.

The Commissioner, however, contended third-party arbitration was the improper route for such an appeal. He believed for this type of incident where the conduct took place "on the playing court," the Commissioner is the final arbiter of any appeals. Notwithstanding, the arbitration hearing date was set. The NBA refused to appear at the arbitration hearing.

So the hearing proceeded without the NBA present. The grievance arbitrator determined:

(1) the CBA gave the grievance arbitrator the authority to determine the arbitrability;

(2) the dispute was in fact arbitrable because the conduct at issue did not take place "on the playing court" (thus, the Commissioner did not have the final say); and

(3) the Commissioner had "just cause" for his suspensions of Artest, Jackson, and Johnson; but that

(4) O'Neal's suspension was too long. (He reduced O'Neal's suspension from twenty-five to fifteen games.)

Meanwhile, the NBA filed a declaratory judgment action in the U.S. District Court for the Southern District of New York.

The gist of the NBA's argument to the district court judge can be summarized as follows:

Look. We get it. The NBA Constitution and the CBA provide the players with procedures to follow if a player is displeased, to put it mildly, with discipline imposed by the Commissioner. In general, the player has the right to have a neutral arbitrator hear his concerns. However, the NBA and the union agreed via the CBA[6] that for conduct, like this that took place "on the playing court"[7] an appeal for such discipline must be taken directly to the Commissioner. The player may not pass go, may not collect $200, may not arbitrate it.

Not surprisingly, the union disagreed with the NBA's interpretation of the CBA. Most notably, the union argued that the conduct did not take place "on the playing court" and was thus appealable to a grievance arbitrator.

Where Does the Term "On the Playing Court" Come From?

Section 35(d) of the NBA Constitution gives the Commissioner broad authority to impose discipline "at or during a game" if the conduct is against the best interests of basketball. However, Section 35(h) of the NBA Constitution gives the players the right to appeal any discipline imposed pursuant to Section 35(d) (except wagering on games) to a grievance arbitrator pursuant to the grievance procedures set forth in the CBA then in effect.

The grievance procedures that were in effect at the time could be found in Section 8 of the CBA and provided an exception to the right to appeal set forth in Section 35(h) of the constitution. Basically, Section 8 read that for a fine or suspension imposed upon a player by the Commissioner for conduct "on the playing court," the Commissioner has final decisionmaking authority.

So the NBA took the position that "misconduct at or dur-

---

6. 1999 CBA.
7. Section 8 of Article XXXI of 1999 CBA provides the language.

ing a game" as used in the Section 35(d) of the NBA Constitution meant the same thing as conduct "on the playing court" as set forth in Section 8 of the CBA. Ultimately it argued that this meant that the Commissioner has the final decisionmaking authority with regard to punishment he imposes "at or during a game" or "on the playing court."

The union didn't believe that was the case. It contended that conduct "on the playing court" about which the Commissioner has the final say, only applies to conduct that occurs as a part of the playing of the game, like flagrant fouls, fights between players, players confronting referees. It does not include discipline for player interactions with fans.

To determine the parties' intended meaning of "on the playing court" versus "at or during a game"—and whether the appeal should thus go to arbitration or to the Commissioner, the district court reviewed:

    (1) the applicable contracts (the CBA, the NBA Constitution, and the Uniform Player Contract);

    (2) Player conduct memos; and

    (3) Past grievances.

First, the district court reviewed the contracts.

Reading Sections 35 (d) and (h) of the NBA Constitution together, with Section 8 of the CBA, the court deduced that the parties could not have intended for the terminology "at or during a game" to be synonymous with "on the playing court." The court based this finding on the fact that each phrase was followed by a clause specifying where such discipline may be challenged. That is, discipline for conduct "at or during a game" can be challenged to an arbitrator, and discipline for conduct "on the playing court" must only be challenged before the Commissioner. If the phrases meant the same thing, then it follows that they would have had the same appeal procedure.

The judge further noted that both parties had sophisticated lawyers. He figured that the lawyers would have used the same terminology if they had wanted to make the provisions have the same meaning. Thus, they must have selected different words in the different provisions for a reason.

To further support that point, the court reviewed the gambling provisions from Section 35(g) of the NBA Constitution and Section 5(e) of the Uniform Player Contract (UPC). Those provisions stated that when it comes to gambling and wagering on games, the Commissioner shall have the power in his sole discretion to discipline the player, and that his finding and decision are "final, binding, conclusive and unappealable."

The court reasoned that the gambling provisions reiterated the point that when the parties want to define absolute authority, they do so.

Lastly, as far as the contracts go, the court observed that the CBA, the NBA Constitution, and the UPC all used the phrases "on the court," "off the court," and "at or during a game," to differentiate among different places where conduct occurs. The court analyzed that this use of different language further showed that the parties meant to distinguish certain conduct.

The court next reviewed the Player Conduct Memos that the NBA had sent to the players each year since 1997. A Player Conduct Memo includes a summary of duties and obligations with respect to conduct on and off the playing court. The applicable year's Memo dictated that violence would not be tolerated on the court and off the court. It broke down different disciplinary actions for "on the court" and "off the court" conduct.

Based on the breakdowns in the memo, the court determined that fighting or striking a fan has never been characterized as conduct "on the playing court" because it is in the section titled "violence off the court."

Thus, the district court decided that O'Neal's actions, which involved shoving an arena employee and punching a spectator, fell into the category of violence "off the court" as defined in the Memo.

Finally, the court reviewed past player grievances.

The NBA argued that the history of grievances between the parties illuminated the union's acknowledgment and understanding that "conduct on the playing court" includes conduct in such off-the-floor locations as the "bench area, the press area, the scorer's table, exit tunnels, the spectator area and even the locker rooms."

The NBA claimed that these prior acknowledgments supported its contention that the incident involving O'Neal was conduct "on the playing court," and was just as inarbitrable as similar conduct for which players were previously disciplined.

The court shook its head at this argument as well. It found that that each of the examples raised by the NBA—of conduct not subject to appeal by arbitration—was specifically defined by the Memo as "on the playing court." The current conduct did not fall within the definition.

The court denied the NBA's motion to vacate the grievance arbitrator's award and granted the union's motion to confirm the grievance arbitrator's award. It was not asked to determine the merits regarding the reduction in O'Neal's suspension.

The NBA and union amended and clarified Section 8 of the next CBA. The 2005 CBA expressly gave the Commissioner final say on "any conduct in the arena" with authority to issue up to twelve-game suspensions,[8] making the current CBA the primary source for the Commissioner's authority.

---

8. *See* NBA Collective Bargaining Agreement Ratified and Signed Posted Jul 30 2005 1:16AM found at http://www.nba.com/news/CBA_050730.html. *See also* nbpa.org for § 8 of the 2005 CBA.

To the Hoop 9

Green Peace

Jon Green, the Detroit fan who threw the Diet Coke on Artest, was convicted of misdemeanor assault for punching Artest and was sentenced to thirty days in jail and two years' probation. He was banished for life from Detroit's home games.[1]

Artest sat out the rest of the 2003–2004 season. He now plays for the Lakers. He has since changed his name to Metta World Peace. "Metta is going to be the first name and it means like friendship, love and kindness," Artest told journalist Stephen A. Smith in September 2011.[2] It is unclear how that is working out, considering he was suspended again in 2012 for elbowing Oklahoma City's James Harden.[3]

For other cases regarding Commissioner authority as to player discipline see *Sprewell v. Golden State Warriors*, 266 F.3d 979 (9th Cir. 2001), and *Molinas v. Nat'l Basketball Ass'n*, 190 F. Supp. 241 (S.D.N.Y. 1961). The preeminent case on Commissioner authority comes from baseball. *See Finley v. Kuhn*, 569 F.2d 527 (7th Cir. 1978).

---

1. *See* http://sports.espn.go.com/nba/news/story?id=4670842 (last visited Sept. 5, 2012).

2. Dave McMenamin, *Ron Artest Now Metta World Peace*, Sept. 16, 2011, espnlosangeles.com. *See* http://espn.go.com/los-angeles/nba/story/_/id/6977866/los-angeles-lakers-ron-artest-name-now-officially-metta-world-peace (last visited Sept. 5, 2012).

3. *See* http://espn.go.com/los-angeles/nba/story/_/id/7851983/metta-world-peace-los-angeles-lakers-suspended-7-games-elbow (last visited Sept. 5, 2012). For the record World Peace claimed it was unintentional.

Chapter 10

Stepping into the High-tops:

Prospective NBA Players and the Collective Bargaining Agreement

Wood v. NBA, 602 F. Supp. 525 (S.D.N.Y. 1984), *aff'd*, 809 F.2d 954 (2d Cir. 1987)

L eon Wood set scoring and assists records as a point guard at Cal State Fullerton in the '80s. In the summer of 1984, he competed in Los Angeles alongside Michael Jordan and Patrick Ewing on the 1984 gold medal-winning USA Olympic basketball team. Also, in the summer of 1984, he was drafted in the first round of the NBA college draft by the Philadelphia 76ers with the 10th pick.

Unfortunately for Wood, at the time of the draft, the 76ers were "over the cap." This means that their team payroll exceeded the amount permitted under the salary cap rule agreed to by the NBA and the National Basketball Players Association in its then-effective Memorandum of Understanding. This didn't mean the 76ers couldn't take on a new draft pick, it just meant that they could only offer him a one-year contract for $75,000. (In comparison, under the 2012 Collective Bargaining Agreement, the 10th pick in the 2012 draft made $1,865,300 in his first season. In addition, agents can plug their rookie client's added value and teams can pay the rookies up to 20 percent more than this minimum. Moreover, under the 2012 CBA, every team has the ability to sign its first round pick on the rookie scale.)

In addition, under the college draft rules in effect in 1984, once a team made an offer to its draft pick, that team held his rights for a year, precluding him from negotiating for a higher salary with any other team during that time.

Wood challenged that call in a federal court.

Prior to the start of the '84 season, Wood refused to sign the contract with Philadelphia and sought to enjoin the NBA and the NBPA's enforcement of the salary cap and the college draft.

He believed the Memorandum did not apply to him. He wanted to negotiate with other teams that could offer him the fair market value for his services. He argued that the Memorandum containing the salary cap and college draft provisions violated Section 1 of the Sherman Act because it constituted an agreement to restrain trade in that it restrained his ability to negotiate with other teams.

The district court held that the salary cap and college draft provisions were exempt from the antitrust laws under the nonstatutory labor exemption because they "[1] affect only the parties to the collective bargaining agreement—the NBA and the players—[2] involve mandatory subjects of bargaining as defined by federal labor laws, and [3] are the result of bona fide arms-length negotiations."[1]

Wood argued that he was a "non-veteran" player and was not within the bargaining unit represented by the NBPA. Basically, he argued that since he was not an NBA player when the union and owners reached agreement on the salary cap, its limits didn't apply to him.

---

1. *Wood v. NBA*, 602 F. Supp. 525, 528.

The court disagreed. It ruled that there is no authority for his proposition and that to adopt such a principle would "turn federal labor policy on its head."

At the time an agreement is signed between the owners and the players' exclusive bargaining representative, all players within the bargaining unit and those who enter the bargaining unit during the life of the agreement are bound by its terms. As the NBPA is the recognized exclusive bargaining agent for NBA players, and he is now an NBA player, the NBPA is his sole representative.

When an employee is hired after the collective bargaining agreement has been made, "the terms of [his] employment already have been traded out." "[T]he duty to bargain is a continuing one, and a union may legitimately bargain over wages and conditions of employment which will affect employees who are to be hired in the future."[2]

Thus, the prospective players step into the shoes of the current ones.

On appeal, Wood emphasized that his superior abilities as a point guard and his selection in the first round of the college draft show that he would have received a higher salary if he had the opportunity to bargain individually. He contended that the CBA (by this time the memorandum had been approved as the new CBA) disadvantages new employees and favors those already hired. Finally, he again argued that it affects those outside the bargaining unit and therefore should not apply to him.

But the 2d Circuit blew the whistle on those arguments. In affirming the district court, the 2d Circuit focused on the fact that the restrictions were "embodied in a collective bargaining agreement between an employer or employers and a labor

---

2. 602 F. Supp. 525.

To the Hoop 10

The Final Call

After playing in the NBA with six different teams over the course of six seasons, Leon Wood became the third NBA player to become an NBA referee.[1]

1. Wood found his calling by picking up a whistle by Jerry Crowe, Feb. 9, 2009, *see* http://articles.latimes.com/2009/feb/09/sports/sp-crowe9 (last visited Sept. 8, 2012).

organization reached through procedures mandated by federal labor legislation." Without probing the exact "contours of the so-called statutory or non-statutory 'labor exemptions,'" as the district court had done, the 2d Circuit found that Wood's claim was a "wholesale subversion" of fundamental principles of federal labor policy under the National Labor Relations Act and outside the purview of the antitrust laws.

It held that one of the fundamental principles of federal labor policy is the legal rule that allows one elected representative to seek the best deal for the greatest number, even if that means favoring those with seniority. Once that representative is chosen, the individual employees cannot negotiate directly with their employer.

Wood had argued that he was outside of that bargaining unit since he had not entered the union when the agreement was made. The 2d Circuit found fault in that argument.

The court emphasized that if newcomers to a bargaining unit could essentially argue that their individual needs were not met (such as Wood's arguments based on his superior abilities and that he would be paid more absent the salary cap), "federal labor policy would essentially collapse, unless a wholly unprincipled, judge-made exception were created for professional athletes."

Finally, the 2d Circuit underscored the importance of freedom of contract in national labor policy. It wrote that freedom of contract (1) allows the parties to make agreements that meet their particular interests and (2) furthers the goal of labor peace. Basically, if the players' unions and the teams can't be allowed to form their own set of compromises, it would lead to a lot more discord and disruption in the sport and "increase the chances of strikes."

If he felt he was discriminated against for being a new employee, the court said, the proper action would be one for breach of the duty of fair representation against the NBPA.

Before his appeal was heard, Wood signed a contract with the 76ers for $1.02 million over four years.

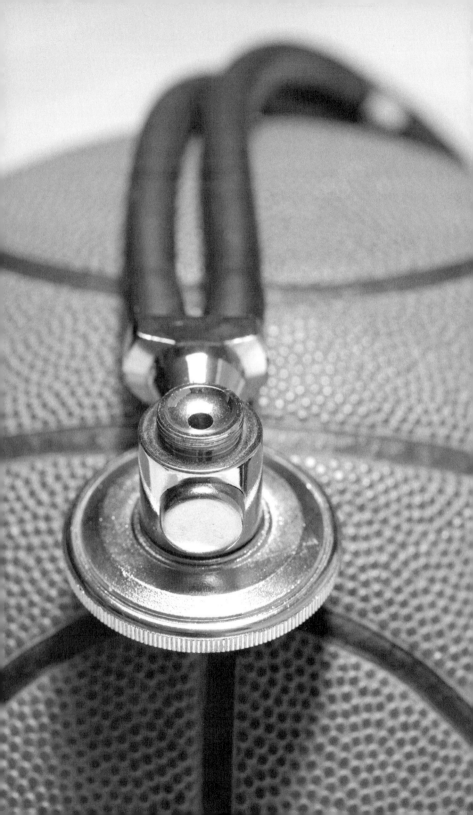

Chapter 11

Team Fouls:
Too Much Trauma

TIG Insurance Co. v. Workers' Compensation Appeals Board and David Feitl, No. A115978, WCAB No. ANA 373705, 2007 WL 2341598, 72 Cal. Comp. Cases 536 (1st Dist. Ct. App.) (WCAB 2007)

I n what state can a professional basketball player file to collect workers' compensation for life from an out-of-state team even if the player was not injured while playing in that state?

California.

And so goes the story of David Feitl.

Feitl played professional basketball in the NBA from 1986 to 1992 with the Houston Rockets, the Golden State Warriors, the Washington Wizards, and the New Jersey Nets. During his last two years in the NBA, he played eight games, plus practices, in California with Houston and one game, plus eight practices, in California with the Nets. Just to put it in perspective—that is nine games in California out of more than 160 total games played throughout the country. After leaving the Nets in 1992, he had some unsuccessful contract wrangling with the Los Angeles Clippers[1] and eventually left the NBA to play for teams in Argentina and France.

---

1. *David Feitl v. Los Angeles Clippers*, 48 F.3d 1227 (1995) (unpublished disposition).

Feitl retired from professional basketball in 1994, citing knee problems.[2] After ending his basketball career, he took on some post-sports career jobs, including ownership of a car wash and sales for an insulation company.

In 2003, he learned some interesting news when a friend told him about California's Labor Code. The California Labor Code has a cumulative trauma statute (Cal. Lab. Code § 5500) that requires an employer that exposes an employee to a physically traumatic activity in California to pay for an employee's lifetime of cumulative trauma (Cal. Lab. Code § 3208.1).

Cumulative trauma is the collective impact of an employee's physically traumatic activity over the course of his career performing that activity.

The California Workers' Compensation Appeals Board has accepted the repeated movement of playing basketball as a physically traumatic activity. This means that a professional basketball player can recover monetary damages for the cumulative impact of his basketball career.

Over the course of his basketball-playing career, Feitl sustained various injuries and surgeries. So, he filed a cumulative injury claim with the WCAB. He claimed he was exposed to cumulative trauma over the course of his career, which included "injury to his knees, shoulders, left groin, elbows, low back, minor left wrist, ankles, neck, and feet." None of the ensuing WCAB decisions indicated that any of these injuries actually occurred in California.

Instead, the workers' compensation judge's (WCJ) decision focused on whether Feitl's injuries came exclusively from basketball or also from nonindustrial factors like his car-washing

---

2. *David Feitl v. Houston Rockets, Golden State Warriors, Washington Wizards, New Jersey Nets, TIG Insurance Co.*, Findings, Award and Order, Case No. *ANA 373705*, 2006 WL 5878326 (WCAB) Aug. 29, 2006.

or insulation sales businesses. Finding that Feitl's injuries only came from basketball, the WCJ held the NBA teams liable for his basketball-related cumulative trauma for the span of his career (including his time spent playing for non-U.S. teams).

The WCJ awarded Feitl permanent disability compensation of $148 per week for 446.75 weeks, starting July 2, 1994, his last day of play in France. In addition, after payment of disability, he would receive a lifetime pension of $19.79 per week.

Feitl was to recover all of it from the Nets (or their insurance carrier), as the Nets were the last team Feitl played for before leaving the NBA. At a later point, the Nets could institute contribution proceedings against other defendants pursuant to Cal. Lab. Code § 5500.5(e).

In addition, the WCJ noted the code's statute of limitations. As none of the NBA teams who employed Feitl provided him with notice of his right to claim workers' compensation benefits in California, despite providing him with significant medical treatment for his injuries, they could not claim the code's one year from injury statute of limitations as a defense.

Not surprisingly, the Nets didn't like the decision. Under the California Labor Code, an employer has two avenues of recourse after an adverse decision: (1) it may file a petition for reconsideration with the WCAB to which a WCJ will provide a recommendation that the WCAB can accept or reject; and then, (2) if that proves unfavorable, the employer may file a writ with the California Court of Appeal to review only for clear error.

Unfortunately for the teams, both shots (of recourse) were air balls. However, to sports lawyers looking for some answers, the decisions in the Nets' appeals have clarified two doctrines that have developed from the statute: the "relation-back" doctrine and the concept of "apportionment."

"Relation Back"

Section 5500.5 of the California Labor Code provides that **liability is limited to the employer in the year preceding an injury** or the **last date of employment resulting in cumulative injury**. However, if the employer during the last year of injurious exposure is "illegally uninsured," then liability is imposed on the **employer during the last year of insured employment that caused exposure** (emphasis added). Hence, liability relates back.

In their petition for reconsideration, the Nets argued that employers are only "illegally uninsured" if (1) they fail to carry the required insurance and (2) California has personal jurisdiction over them.[3]

If there is no jurisdiction, they are merely uninsured, *not illegally* uninsured. Since the WCAB did not have jurisdiction over the European teams, those teams were not illegally uninsured and the WCAB should have looked to see whether they were insured before imposing such sweeping liability on the Nets.

Feitl disagreed. He countered that it is not necessary to look to whether the European teams were insured, unless California has jurisdiction over them. So, instead of looking to whether an employer is "illegally uninsured," he argued the board should just look to whether there is jurisdiction. He argued that where the employer during the employee's last year of injurious exposures is one over whom the board does not have jurisdiction, such as a European team, then liability relates back to the immediately preceding employer over whom the board has jurisdiction.[4] Since there was no evidence that the board had

---

3. Petition for Reconsideration, Case No. ANA 03737, 2006 WL 5878329 (CA WCAB Docs) Sept. 26, 2006.

4. Applicant/Respondent's Answer to Defendant's Petition for Reconsideration, 2006 WL 5878330 (CA WCAB Docs) Oct. 4, 2006.

jurisdiction over teams in France or Argentina, liability related back to the immediately preceding employer over which the board did have jurisdiction: the New Jersey Nets.

The recommending judge agreed with Feitl. In addressing the Nets' contention that the board should look to whether the foreign teams have insurance, he concluded that California must first have jurisdiction over an employer before it assigns it any liability. And since California did not have jurisdiction over the teams in France, Italy, and Argentina, it need not look to whether those teams had workers' compensation insurance.[5]

Apportionment

Okay, if liability relates back to the team over which California had jurisdiction, the Nets contended that at least that liability should be divided equitably among all employers over which California had jurisdiction. It really isn't fair that one team must pay for cumulative injuries over the span of the player's career.

The Nets asserted that Section 4663 of the California Labor Code supported their argument. It provides that apportionment of disability must be based on causation, and should be read together with Section 4664, which provides that an employer is only liable for the percentage of disability directly caused by injury occurring in the course of employment. The Nets thus maintained that as they did not cause Feitl's post-NBA injuries, they should not be liable for those injuries. All the liability should be apportioned fairly among those who did cause the injuries.

Feitl responded that that Sections 4663 and 4664 of the California Labor Code do not require apportionment as to the player. He asserted that at the time that the California legislature enacted those sections the legislators could have also amended

---

5. Report and Recommendation on Petition for Reconsideration, Case No. ANA 313705, 2006 WL 5878327 (CA WCAB Docs) Oct. 6, 2006.

the relation-back doctrine to specifically address apportionment and override Section 5500's relation-back doctrine, and they had not done so.

The judge considered the history of the applicable labor codes. Briefly, in April 2004, the California legislature overhauled California workers' compensation with Bill SB 899.

Prior to SB 899, a cumulative injury would be evaluated as follows:

> (1) determine overall permanent disability under Section 4660;

> (2) determine apportionment to nonindustrial factors under Section 4663; and

> (3) determine which employers are liable under Section 5500.5(a).

Among its changes, SB899 amended Section 4663 and added Section 4664 to the second step above. The relevant part provides: "the employer shall only be liable for the percentage of permanent disability directly caused by the injury."

Because Section 4664 did not limit the recoverable cumulative trauma to injuries sustained during the period of employment by an employer, the judge concluded that the legislature must have equated "injury" with "cumulative trauma" that occurred during employment with all industry employers.

And since it was all one industry, any one of the employers caused the cumulative trauma. Since none of the injuries was found to be due to nonindustrial factors, 100 percent of the applicant's permanent disability was caused by cumulative injury and the last "industry" employer under California's jurisdiction is liable.

He concluded that Section 5500.5 determines liability for cumulative injuries, while Sections 4663 and 4664 deal with the separate issue of apportionment among the teams once liability is assigned. They are not meant to reduce an employee's recovery. The judge thus agreed with Feitl that Section 5500.5(a) allocates liability among employers only once an employer is found liable to the employee.

But the Nets found that unreasonable. They argued that since California has no jurisdiction over the European teams, the Nets will have a difficult time instituting any apportionment proceedings against them. The Nets will be unduly burdened with paying more than their fair share of Feitl's reward by taking on the full liability for the cumulative injury, even though injurious exposure in California was tenuous at best—it consisted of Feitl's participation in only one game for less than ten minutes and eight practices within the state of California.

The Nets further argued that this would make California the forum of choice for employees who believe they have sustained cumulative trauma over the course of their career no matter how little occurred in that state.

Their arguments were to no avail. The judge recommended that the petition for reconsideration be denied, based on:

(1) California's lack of jurisdiction over the foreign teams: because the board had no jurisdiction over the European teams, and the Nets were Feitl's employer during the last year when injurious employment took place, they were responsible for the cumulative trauma that spanned his career;

(2) the provision's statutory history; and

(3) the public policy that an employee should receive all of his benefits even if it means that one party must take on all accountability. Instead of reducing or delaying a worker's recovery, the burden of seeking apportionment is on a liable party.

To the Hoop 11

Case Typical but
Change on the Horizon

Regardless of which side you take—that of the players: that they should only need to track down one employer to collect compensation for the trauma they sustained from their cumulative basketball injuries; or that of the employer: that it is an injustice that one out-of-state employer must pay the costs of California workers' compensation when the employee only had tenuous California contacts in the first place—the issue is not going away. Feitl's case is typical.

However, recently, NFL teams that have included forum selection clauses in their contracts to ensure that workers' compensation claims are limited to the club's forum state have found limited success. Federal district courts in Ohio and Georgia as well as the 9th Circuit held that showing tenuous California contacts, without showing specific injury in California, was not enough to vacate an arbitration award denying relief under the California cumulative trauma statute. *See Cincinnati Bengals, Inc. v. Abdullah*, 2013 WL 154077, (S.D. Ohio 2013) ("None of the Players have set forth facts establishing that they sustained a specific or particular injury in California, or that they received any care in that state as a result."); *Atlanta Falcons Football Club LLC v. National Football League Players Ass'n*, 2012 WL 5392185 (N.D. Ga. 2012) ("The Players have not shown an 'explicit, well-defined, and dominant public policy' in California against arbitral awards enforcing agreements to seek workers' compensation benefits in Georgia instead of in California when the Players only have a limited connection with California."); and *Matthews v. National Football League Management Council*, 688 F.3d 1107, 193 L.R.R.M. (BNA) 3126 (9th Cir. 2012) ("We hold that Matthews has not alleged sufficient contacts with California to show that his workers' compensation claim comes within the scope of California's workers' compensation regime.").

In addition, California Assemblyman Henry Perea

introduced Bill 1309, Feb. 25, 2013, that would preclude out-of-state professional athletes from seeking California workers' compensation from their out-of-state employers. See http://www.insurancejournal.com/news/west/2013/03/01/283346.htm (last visited March 18, 2013).

Following the judge's recommendation, the Nets pursued their second avenue of recourse and requested a writ to set aside the order denying their petition.

They wanted a federal court to determine whether a professional basketball player who played for teams based outside of California and outside of the United States should be permitted to obtain from only one team (that was not even a California team) California workers' compensation benefits for injuries that did not necessarily occur in California and that spanned the proballer's entire basketball career. They wanted the court to relinquish jurisdiction over out-of-state teams and injuries.

In finding for Feitl, the 1st District Court of Appeal was not to be persuaded. The court applied the relation-back doctrine. It held that, if California does not have jurisdiction over the player's last team, the player can make a claim against his last team over which California does exercise jurisdiction. As to apportionment, the court ruled that because apportionment relates to the teams only, the player need not go after each employer. The player can recover from one team and then the teams can work it out among themselves.

Chapter 12

Incidental Contact?

Sexual Harassment in the Front Office

Sanders v. Madison Square Garden, L.P.,
101 Fair Empl. Prac. Cas. (BNA) 390, 2007 WL 2254698
(S.D.N.Y. 2007), not reported in F. Supp. (*MSG I*);
Sanders v. Madison Square Garden, L.P.,
525 F. Supp. 2d 364 (S.D.N.Y. 2007) (*MSG II*)

Anucha Browne Sanders started work for the New York Knicks in 2000 as the vice president for marketing and business operations. She was in charge of promoting the Knicks and heading up their communications programs, game presentations, and community events.

After working for the Knicks for two years, she received glowing reviews and a major promotion to oversee not only the Knicks' promotions but also its business operations. Browne Sanders continued to receive high performance reviews. That, is until 2004.

In 2003, the Knicks hired former Detroit Piston and Hall of Famer Isiah Lord Thomas as president of basketball operations, overseeing coaches and players. Although Thomas did not supervise Browne Sanders, she kept him informed about business developments related to the team. But they did not work well together.

Soon after Thomas was hired, as Browne Sanders later alleged in a sexual harassment complaint, Thomas "took pains" to marginalize her and prevent her from doing her job.[1] For example, after the Knicks lost a game following a community event that she planned, "Thomas announced that the players would no longer be required to do any community events. Soon after his announcement, Thomas grabbed [her] arm and pulled her into a small room to the side of the team's locker room. He yelled that the team was not going to do 'any more f--king events.'"

She also alleged that during this time Thomas berated her and called her a "bitch" and a "ho" and told her she could no longer speak to his basketball staff or Knicks players directly. Since communicating with the basketball staff and the players was a crucial part of her job responsibilities, she asked her supervisor how she could do her job in light of Thomas's restrictions. According to her eventual legal complaint, her supervisor told her to accommodate Thomas.

Browne Sanders further contended in her complaint that throughout the late spring and summer of 2004, Thomas continued to make it difficult for her to perform her job. She alleged that he acted in a hostile manner toward her, refused to engage in sales-related activities that she planned and told his staff and the Knicks players not to take direction from "that bitch."

She further wrote in her complaint, that by December 2004, Thomas changed his antics by making sexual advances toward her. She wrote that he repeatedly professed his love for her and even compared his feelings for her to the movie *Love and Basketball*. She also said that he made comments about her physical appearance, and suggested that they go "offsite" together. In her complaint, she wrote that she told her supervisor about this behavior as well, but he did not respond.

---

1. *Sanders v. Madison Square Garden, LP, Isiah Lord Thomas, and James L. Dolan*, Nov. 10, 2006. Second Amended Complaint 2006 WL 3887257.

She contended that when she declined his advances, Thomas continued to try to undermine her ability to do her job.[2] For example, she said that she had to resort to using cardboard cutouts of Knicks players to promote the team because Thomas would not make the players available to her.

To that point, Thomas agreed that they "butted heads" because he wanted complete control over players' time and responsibilities and she wanted to meet with players for media and promotional obligations."[3]

By the end of 2005, she started documenting his actions toward her and asked others to document any forms of behavior they felt was inappropriately directed toward them. After having made several informal complaints to her superiors, Browne Sanders's attorney met with Madison Square Garden's (MSG) counsel (MSG is the parent company of the New York Knicks) to discuss her internal complaint. MSG agreed to conduct an in-house investigation of her claims, but told her she couldn't go to work during that time. During MSG's internal review process, both Browne Sanders and Thomas were interviewed and the parties discussed a settlement of the claims.

After completing its internal investigation, in January 2006, the then-acting general counsel for MSG drafted a memo for the senior vice president of human resources.

The memo recommended that Thomas receive "sensit[ivity]" training, in light of the finding that Thomas "occasion[ally] used profanity and . . . raised his voice in the workplace," and to address "one occasion" on which Thomas "greeted Browne Sanders with a hug and kiss."

The memo also stated that "most of Browne Sanders's alle-

2. 2007 WL 3144545 (S.D.N.Y.) (Verdict and Settlement Summary) (Oct. 4, 2007).

3. *Sanders v. Madison Square Garden, LP*, 101 Fair Empl.Prac.Cas. (BNA) 390, 2007 WL 2254698 (S.D.N.Y. Aug. 6, 2007), not reported in F. Supp. (*MSG I*).

gations were not confirmed," she had exhibited a "poor relationship and [had] difficulty interacting with . . . members of MSG management," and that Browne Sanders and Thomas had a "number of business disagreements in philosophy and management style."

Most significantly, the memo recommended: "[I]n light of . . . issues related to . . . Browne Sanders' communication skills and overall effectiveness, Browne Sanders' employment should be terminated." So, on January 19, 2006, Browne Sanders was dismissed from her employment with the Knicks.

Getting fired after complaining about sexual harassment did not go over too well with Browne Sanders. Five days later, she sued MSG, its president, James L. Dolan, and Thomas in the U.S. District Court for the Southern District of New York. The gist of her claims was that (1) she was discriminated against on the basis of her sex and (2) she was terminated in retaliation for complaining about it.

Because none of the parties moved for summary judgment on the sex discrimination claim, the court did not discuss its merits. It left that claim for the jury to decide. Instead, it focused on Browne Sanders's retaliation claim.

A retaliation claim is a claim that an employer has fired an employee, or taken other adverse action against an employee, because the employee complained about the employer's illegal activities (or alleged illegal activities), or the employee engaged in other forms of protected activity. (Think, *The Insider.*)

To make a prima facie case of retaliation, Browne Sanders needed to show that:

    (1) she engaged in a protected activity;

    (2) MSG was aware that she engaged in a protected activity;

    (3) she suffered an adverse employment action; and

(4) there was a causal connection between the protected activity and the adverse action.

To defend a retaliation claim, MSG needed to show that Browne Sanders (1) did not engage in a protected activity or (2) that there was no causal connection between her complaint and her firing—that they fired her for legitimate, nonretaliatory reasons.

Browne Sanders's sexual harassment complaint was only a protected activity if she truly believed sexual harassment took place. This did not mean at this stage that she needed to establish that Thomas actually sexually harassed her. She just needed to establish that she reasonably thought he did.

In response to Browne Sanders's motion for summary judgment on the retaliation claim, MSG contended that Browne Sanders could not have had a good-faith belief that Thomas sexually harassed her. They supported this stance by proffering evidence that she was only after money. They noted that she did not complain about Thomas's behavior until she thought her job was in jeopardy; she offered to settle her claim for around $6 million; and she threatened to go public with her lawsuit if MSG failed to agree to such a settlement.

The court found MSG's evidence persuasive and held that it could not say as a matter of law that her belief was honest and bona fide. The court thus denied Browne Sanders's motion and held that a jury should determine whether her contentions of sexual harassment were genuine and therefore protected.

Next, assuming Browne Sanders engaged in a legitimate protected activity (they can file their response in the alternative not knowing how the court will rule on the first issue), MSG argued that it fired Browne Sanders for other reasons—legitimate, nonretaliatory reasons.

MSG claimed it fired her because she: (1) pressured subordinates to support her case and (2) attempted to "extort" money from MSG by making false accusations concerning sexual harassment.

The court found that these were also questions of fact for the jury to decide. To help guide its decision, the court wrote that the jury could consider evidence of the settlement discussions: the jury will have to consider whether her settlement demands were legitimate or were an attempt to secure an extortionate settlement, as the defendants contended.

Thus, the court denied Browne Sanders's motion for partial summary judgment on the retaliation issue. This meant she would need to prove to a jury that she was in fact sexually harassed and had a good-faith belief she was sexually harassed and was fired for reporting it.

Reconsideration

Browne Sanders asked the court to reconsider her motion for summary judgment on the retaliation issue, arguing that (1) the court was incorrect in its application of the retaliation statute and (2) that it should not submit any evidence of settlement negotiations to the jury.

In agreeing to rehear her case, the court reiterated the elements of retaliation from its first opinion: For Browne Sanders's complaint to receive protection from retaliation, she needed to have a good-faith belief that she was sexually harassed. If she just made up the claims to extort money from MSG, well, then that would not be protected.

With respect to its earlier opinion, the court admitted that it had made a mistake to hold that where an employee acted in good faith but the employer believed the employee was engaged in bad-faith behavior, the employer's belief could be a defense to retaliation. The court said it is not up to an employer to unilaterally determine whether an employee's claim was made in good or bad faith—that is for the jury to decide. "Many employers do believe the claims made by their employees are completely without merit," the court said, "but the law requires the employer to tolerate such complaints and not to retaliate because of them."[4]

The court went on to write that if an employer can fire an employee any time the employer believed the employee's complaints were unfounded or malicious, the protection asserted in Title VII would be illusory. (See *To the Hoop 12* on Title VII.)

It held that as long as the employee in good faith believes the employer has discriminated against him/her—even if the employer's behavior does not actually violate Title VII—the behavior is protected. If an employer fires the employee for making false or bad-faith accusations, it does so at its own risk that a jury will disagree with that characterization.

In addition, the court found that any efforts to document what Browne Sanders believed were illegal activities were also protected.

Browne Sanders had also asked the court to reconsider whether testimony relating to the settlement negotiations was admissible. The initial summary judgment opinion suggested that evidence of a demand of a large sum of money was relevant to the issue of her good-faith complaint under Federal Rule of Evidence (FRE) 401.

Upon reconsideration, the court examined FRE 408(a), which prohibits evidence of settlement negotiations to prove the validity of the underlying claim.

Browne Sanders had made two claims: a claim that Thomas

---

4. *Sanders v. MSG*, 525 F. Supp. 2d 364, 367 (Spring 2007) (*MSG II*).

sexually harassed her (Claim 1) and a claim that she was fired in retaliation for her complaints about the harassment (Claim 2).

Since the settlement offer was made to settle Claim 1, the sexual harassment claim, FRE 408(a) would prohibit any evidence of her settlement demand to disprove that claim.

On the other hand, the court recognized that the settlement offer was not made to settle Claim 2, the retaliation claim. In fact, there was no retaliation claim to settle at the time of the initial negotiations. She hadn't yet been fired. The settlement negotiations started when MSG began its internal investigation.

MSG wanted to use Browne Sanders's settlement offer as evidence not to refute the sexual harassment allegations in Claim 1, but as a defense to the retaliation claim in Claim 2.

MSG believed that the settlement offer would prove that Browne Sanders did not in fact engage in a protected activity. The way it wanted to show that was to say that her underlying sexual harassment claim was made in bad faith, as evidenced by the extortionate amount of money she asked for in a settlement. Since her activity was not protected, MSG did not fire her for engaging in a protected activity.

The court didn't buy it.

The court said that the evidence was offered for the forbidden purpose of showing that the underlying claim of sexual harassment, which was the subject of the settlement discussions, was frivolous.

Further, the court noted that even if the evidence was permitted under FRE 408, it must meet FRE 403's test on probative value—that the probative value of the evidence must exceed any prejudicial impact of the evidence in order to be admissible.

The court found the evidence would have a highly prejudicial impact. It would be very difficult for the jurors to close their ears to the evidence of settlement negotiations as to Claim 1 and only apply it as to Claim 2. The court said that would be "highly confusing" to the jury.

So the court withdrew its original opinion and a month later, a jury found that Thomas harassed Browne Sanders and that MSG and Dolan retaliated by firing her. It determined that her punitive damages totaled $11.6 million. MSG was ordered to pay Browne Sanders $6 million for the sexual harassment she endured and $2.6 million for retaliating against her. Dolan owed the additional $3 million.[5] That was just punitive damages. Before the compensatory damages were decided, the parties settled.[6]

Browne Sanders and Thomas have gone back to the college arena. At the time of publication Browne Sanders is the Vice President of NCAA Women's Basketball Championships[7] and Thomas is completing his Masters Degree at Cal Berkeley.[8]

---

5. 2007 WL 3144545 (S.D.N.Y.) (Verdict and Settlement Summary), Copyright (c) 2012 ALM Media Properties, LLC. United States District Court, S.D. New York, *Anucha Browne Sanders v. Madison Square Garden L.P., Isiah Lord Thomas III, and James L. Dolan*, No. 1:06-cv-00589-GEL-DCF DATE OF VERDICT/SETTLEMENT: Oct. 4, 2007.

6. *See* http://sports.espn.go.com/nba/news/story?id=3149371.

7. http://espn.go.com/blog/new-york/knicks/post/_/id/23216/ncaa-hires-anucha-browne-sanders.

8. http://www.mercurynews.com/cal-bears/ci_21430836/hall-famer-isiah-thomas-walking-halls-at-cal.

To the Hoop 12

Sex Discrimination

Browne Sanders filed a sex discrimination and retaliation suit under New York Human Rights Law and New York Executive Law 296 as well as similar claims under New York's Administrative Code of the City of New York 8-107. The basis of all of the claims was the same: Discrimination based on her sex and retaliation in the form of firing for complaining about it. In addition, she reserved the right to amend the claim to include a federal violation of Title VII of the Civil Rights Act of 1964. Title VII prohibits employment discrimination based on race, color, religion, sex, and national origin. Under the law, before bringing a claim under Title VII, a plaintiff must exhaust her administrative remedies by filing a charge with the Equal Employment Opportunity Commission (EEOC), the federal agency charged with the authority to investigate employment discrimination claims. The agency investigates and either determines that there is cause to believe a violation of the federal discrimination statutes exists, or that there is no cause to make such a determination. If it decides the former, the EEOC will provide the charging party with a notice of a right to sue, after which a plaintiff can file a lawsuit in state or federal court, which is what Browne Sanders did. The EEOC provided her with a notice of right to sue letter on September 21, 2006. She then amended her complaint on November 10, 2006, to include the federal claims. Notably, individuals cannot be liable under Title VII, thus, the claims against Dolan and Thomas were only asserted under state law.

Chapter 13

Outside the Paint:
Spectator Injuries

Geeslin v. Bryant, No. 06-2768-STA,
2010 WL 2365329 (W.D. Tenn. 2010),
rev'd in part, 453 F. App'x 637 (6th Cir. 2011)

B ill Geeslin and a friend attended a game between the Los
Angeles Lakers and the Memphis Grizzlies at the FedEx
Forum in Memphis, Tennessee, on November 14, 2005.
Geeslin had received skybox tickets to the game from a casi-
no; but once he arrived at the skybox, his host offered him an
upgrade. He was moved to folding chairs on the floor just to the
side of one of the baskets in the front row.[1] *Score! Geeslin was
in luck (or maybe not).*

While he was watching the action from his courtside seat,
a Lakers player threw a pass to Kobe Bryant. In his attempt to
catch the ball, Bryant flew out of bounds and fell into Geeslin,
causing him to spill his beer and fall backward. As Bryant got
back to his feet, his forearm went into Geeslin's chest. According to Geeslin, Bryant also glared at him as he moved away, and
did not apologize.[2]

Geeslin eventually sought medical attention for pain in his
chest and was diagnosed with a bruised lung cavity and anxiety
from the incident.

---

1. *Geeslin v. Bryant*, No. 06-2768-STA, 2010 WL 2365329 (W.D. Tenn. June 9, 2010).
2. Reply Brief of Plaintiff-Appellant, *Betty GEESLIN, as Personal Representative
of the Estate of Bill Geeslin, Deceased, Plaintiff-Appellant, v. Kobe BRYANT, Defen-
dant-Appellee*. United States Court of Appeals, 6th Circuit. 2010 WL 6487977 (C.A.6)
(Appellate Brief).

Geeslin felt violated by Bryant, so he charged Bryant with assault, battery, and intentional infliction of emotional distress. Unfortunately, in June 2008, before the case was heard, Geeslin died at the age of forty-nine.

His mother continued the suit on his behalf. In June 2010, five years after the incident and two years after Geeslin's death, the case came before the U.S. District Court for the Western District of Tennessee.

In his deposition, Geeslin had conceded that he may have possibly consented to a player running into him during the game, but he did not consent to being used as a "human punching bag" on Bryant's return to the game.[3]

The district court judge disagreed that the contact could be analyzed in two parts (the fall and the rise) and ruled that by sitting courtside Geeslin consented to the entire contact, not just the first:

> Here, the Plaintiff was sitting on the floor of an NBA basketball game when the Defendant ran into him while trying to keep the ball in play. It is reasonable that in a situation such as this, the Defendant's arms and body in general might come into contact with a spectator like Plaintiff which the Plaintiff himself concedes. It is also reasonable, however, that the Defendant might need to touch or push Plaintiff to get up and back into the game. Thus, the Plaintiff assumed the risk or consented to the entire contact between he and the Defendant.

In other words, "Hey, it's a basketball game. If you sit courtside, you run the risk of a player falling into you."[4]

---

3. *Geeslin v. Bryant*, No. 06-2768-STA, 2010 WL 2365329 (W.D. Tenn. June 9, 2010).

4. For a humorous take on the assumption of risk doctrine, *see* Bill Simmons, *Big Book of Basketball* at 268.

The judge wrote that even if Bryant pushed Geeslin in a frustrated or aggressive manner in an attempt to get back into the game, no reasonable juror could conclude that Bryant intended to cause Geeslin harm. The judge found this lack of intent further evidenced by the fact that nothing indicated the two men had any animosity toward each other or even knew each other.

Thus, the district court judge held that Geeslin, by sitting courtside, assumed the risk of a player falling into him, and there was no evidence of intent by Bryant to cause Geeslin harm. The district court thus granted Bryant summary judgment.

On behalf of her son, Betty Geeslin appealed the district court's decision to the 6th Circuit. In her appeal, she focused on Bryant's state of mind when he reentered the game. Ms. Geeslin believed his mindset would prove the requisite intent.

She argued that the evidence on record supported "a reasonable inference and conclusion that Kobe Bryant acted out of anger and frustration with the intent to harm Bill Geeslin."

She cited her late son's earlier deposition testimony, that Bryant's anger derived from the events in the game that led up to the incident: the Lakers were losing, Bryant was pushed out of bounds on the fast break instead of scoring, and no foul was called on the Grizzlies player who had fouled him. She also asserted that Bryant didn't act the way one would expect after an accidental encounter: "At no time did Kobe Bryant say 'I'm sorry,' 'excuse me,' 'pardon me,' or otherwise apologize or express regret to Bill Geeslin as one would expect a civilized person to do after an accidental or inadvertent physical encounter." Thus, Bryant had the requisite mental state to intentionally forearm her son.

The panel agreed with the district court that there was no dispute that Bryant's initial contact with Geeslin was involun-

To the Hoop 13

Follow the Bouncing Ball

Spectators at basketball games will assume the risk of a ball and possibly a player involuntarily flying into the stands. However, at least in the 6th Circuit, once the involuntary action ends, the player should be aware of his intentional actions.

For a basketball case where a courtside photographer was found to have assumed the risk of injuries, consider *Bereswill v. Nat'l Basketball Ass'n*, 719 N.Y.S.2d 231 (Sup. Ct. 2001). The court in *Bereswill* found that the photographer assumed the risk of sitting courtside in light of his experience and his conduct; any increased risks, the court said, were obvious to him and he fully comprehended the circumstances. In *McFatridge v. Harlem Globe Trotters, 365 P.2d 918* (N.M. 1961), the court said that the fan would assume the risk if she knew or should have known that there was a danger of being struck (by a ball). That case was decided fifty years ago and the popularity of basketball has grown since then, to the point where, arguably, most people know the risks involved with the sport. The fact that the Globe Trotters are more like a choreographed show and less of a competitive game where anything can happen, could differentiate it from the typical "assumption of risk" scenario.

tary, meaning that when he flew out of bounds he lost his balance attempting to get the ball and probably didn't mean to collide with Geeslin.[5]

The court wrote however, that the assumption of risk or consent to contact only applied to the initial contact and not the secondary, offensive conduct as described by Geeslin. It prob-

5. *Geeslin v. Bryant*, 453 F. App'x 637, 640 (2011).

ably didn't help Bryant's case that he "offered neither deposition testimony nor an affidavit in opposition to the motion."[6]

In Tennessee the tort of battery requires an intentional act that causes bodily contact that is unpermitted, harmful, or offensive. When a plaintiff has given consent for the contact or the defendant has a just cause or excuse for the contact, there is no battery. In an unpublished opinion, the 6th Circuit found that there was a genuine issue of material fact as to whether Bryant intentionally injured Geeslin when he was getting up to get back into the game. It remanded the case to determine that intent.

As to the claim of intentional infliction of emotional distress (IIED), the court agreed with the district court's finding summary judgment for Bryant on that account.

In Tennessee, a claim for IIED requires a showing by the plaintiff of:

(1) intentional or reckless conduct;

(2) conduct so outrageous it is not tolerated by civilized society; and

(3) a serious mental injury to plaintiff resulting from the conduct.

A successful claim is limited to "mental injury which is so severe that no reasonable person would be expected to endure it." The court found that the sleeplessness and anxiety that Geeslin described feeling after the incident are not evidence of severe mental injury. In addition, the panel noted "that a rough push by Bryant in leaving the scene of the collision does not reach the level of 'outrageous' behavior sufficient to support such a claim."

The parties settled before the jury trial was scheduled to begin. Perhaps saying sorry is the best defense.

---

6. 453 F. App'x 637, 640 (2011).

Chapter 14

Giving Student-Athletes the Third Degree:

Is Compensation in the Future for College Athletes?

Edward O'Bannon v. Nat'l Collegiate Athletic Ass'n,
No. 09-1967 CW, 2010 WL 445190 (N.D. Cal. 2010)
(Order denying NCAA and CLC's motions to dismiss);
*In re NCAA Student-Athlete Name & Likeness
Licensing Litigation,* 2011 WL 3240518 (N.D. Cal. 2011)
(Order denying EA's motion to dismiss)

E d O'Bannon is leading a team to ensure the answer is yes.

As a forward at UCLA, O'Bannon led the Bruins to a win against Arkansas in the 1995 NCAA Men's Basketball Championship, scooping up a few other accolades along the way. (In that game, O'Bannon scored 30 points and had 17 rebounds.) He received the John R. Wooden award as the nation's most outstanding men's basketball player for the 1994–95 season and the Associated Press selected him as the 1994–95 NCAA tournament's Most Outstanding Player.

Not only may college hoops fans savor the memory of his incredible game, but they can also watch it over and over again by purchasing the game on DVD. That's right, the NCAA's online store sells a two-DVD box set for $39.99. It is described as "Ed O'Bannon, earning MVP honors, led UCLA back to prominence by defeating Arkansas 89–78 for their 11th title in school history."[1]

None of the proceeds from those sales, however, go into O'Bannon's pocket. This is because when he was in college, he signed an agreement (like Form 8-3a noted below) turning over to the NCAA all rights to his college image and likeness for, arguably, perpetuity. But one can't worry about perpetuity when in college. If he wanted to play, he signed on the line.

Jump forward fifteen years. After a short stint in the NBA and some playing time in Europe, O'Bannon now handles sales and promotions for Findlay Toyota in Las Vegas. His basketball-playing days are in his past. He has some posters of that championship team on his walls; there is even a basketball hoop in the parking lot of the dealership, but for the most part, his life is not about basketball anymore.[2]

Then, Sonny Vaccaro tried walking in his shoes.

Vaccaro is "a self-described creator of the 'shoe contract' whereby college coaches were paid by shoe companies in exchange for their players wearing a particular brand of shoe in competition."[3] He orchestrated these deals on behalf of the shoe companies. Vaccaro had a change of heart, you could say, and believed the student-athletes had been treated unfairly by the NCAA.[4] He wanted to help them obtain some of the proceeds

---

1. 2009 WL 2416720 (N.D.Cal.) (Original Trial Pleading).

2. Washington Post, *Ed O'Bannon: From the Hardwood to the Car Lot.* http://www.washingtonpost.com/wpdyn/content/video/2009/05/29/VI2009052901603.html.

3. 2012 WL 2848947 (N.D.Cal.) (Trial Filing), United States District Court, N.D. Cal., Oakland Division, *In re NCAA Student-Athlete Name & Likeness Licensing Litigation,* Nos. 4:09-cv-1967 CW (NC), 3:10-cv-00632-CW (NC), 4:11-cv-00388 CW (NC), 4:11-cv-04938 CW (NC). May 9, 2012. Joint case management conference filing.

4. http://www.pbs.org/wgbh/pages/frontline/money-and-march-madness/ncaa-lawsuit/ (last visited July 18, 2012).

from the sales of their likenesses and regain the rights to their images.

So Vaccaro asked O'Bannon to be the lead plaintiff in such a case, to which O'Bannon was happy to oblige: "My biggest thing right now is, once we leave the university and are done playing in the NCAA, one would think we'd be able to leave with our likeness," O'Bannon has said. "But we aren't able to. If you don't take your likeness with you, you should at least be compensated for every dime that is made off your name or likeness."[5]

O'Bannon was on board, but how were they going to go up against the NCAA?

Initially, O'Bannon filed an antitrust lawsuit on behalf of himself and other former[6] players against the NCAA and the Collegiate Licensing Company (CLC), the licensing arm of the NCAA.

He set forth two main antitrust claims:[7]

> (1) The NCAA and its member institutions' agreement to require student-athletes to relinquish their rights of publicity via Form 8-3a (the agreement that gives NCAA the right to use their images) was an illegal restraint of trade. The requirement to sign the form harmed competition by setting the athletes' compensation at zero. It completely precluded them from competing in the market for collegiate memorabilia. Form 8-3a reads as follow:
>
>> You authorize the NCAA [or a third party acting on behalf of the NCAA (e.g., host institution, con-

---

5. *See* http://www.lostlettermen.com/why-im-fighting-the-ncaa/#d6TeohDjjt806 L2R.99.

6. O'Bannon added current players to the class in August 31, 2012. *In re NCAA Student-Athlete Name & Likeness Licensing Litigation*, 2012 WL 4043912 (N.D. Cal.) (Trial Motion, Memorandum and Affidavit); No. 4:09-cv-1967 CW (NC). Aug. 31, 2012. Notice of Motion and Motion by Antitrust Plaintiffs for Class Certification and Memorandum of Points and Authorities in Support Thereof.

7. 2009 WL 2416720 (N.D.Cal.) (Original Trial Pleading).

ference, local organizing committee)] to use *your name or picture to generally promote NCAA championships or other NCAA events, activities or programs*.

(2) He also argued that the NCAA and its member institutions' agreement with CLC constituted a group boycott or refusal to deal. Their concerted action not only required all student-athletes to sign Form 8-3a each year, but the CLC also promised the NCAA that it would not compensate the student-athletes pursuant to NCAA Bylaw 12.5.1.1.1.

O'Bannon also made a claim for restitution. He argued that the NCAA and CLC were unjustly enriched because they took for themselves the benefits that the class members' rights of publicity conferred. (As we discussed in Chapter Two, the right of publicity protects the misappropriation of a person's identity from commercial use by another. O'Bannon was essentially saying that by using the class members' identities in commercial ventures, the NCAA was profiting off stolen goods.)

The NCAA and CLC each filed motions to dismiss the case, but the U.S. District Court for the Northern District of California denied those requests, finding enough questions of fact to let the case proceed.

Judge Claudia Wilken first looked to the requirements of a claim under Section 1 of the Sherman Act:

(1) a contract, combination, or conspiracy;

(2) that unreasonably restrained trade under either a per se rule of illegality or a rule of reason analysis; and

(3) that the restraint affected interstate commerce.

Prong three was easily shown since the collegiate market is nationwide, but let's take a closer look at the first two prongs.

1. A Contract

The court found that O'Bannon showed that a contract, the NCAA constitution, existed between the NCAA and its member schools. Under Article 3.2.4.6 of the NCAA Constitution, the member schools agreed to require each student-athlete to sign Form 8-3a in order to participate in collegiate athletics.

As to O'Bannon's second claim, the court found that O'Bannon also provided evidence of a contract between the NCAA and CLC, whereby CLC agreed to abide by the NCAA Constitution, which calls for preserving student-athletes' eligibility by not compensating them. Once the NCAA member schools have the athletes sign Form 8-3a, the NCAA, through its licensing representative CLC, makes deals that license products and media containing former NCAA players' images, which do not compensate the former athletes. For example, EA used former athletes in video games under a license from CLC.

2. Unreasonable Restraint

Only unreasonable restraints of trade are illegal. To determine whether an alleged restraint is unreasonable, the court may employ a per se rule of illegality or test the restraint under the rule of reason.

If an agreement is per se illegal, there is no need to conduct a rule of reason analysis. A per se event is rare. It is usually found where there has been an agreement among direct competitors or the court has experience with the restraint at issue.

Because O'Bannon didn't allege an agreement among competitors and the type of price-fixing conspiracy he alleged is novel, the court said that it must subject the complaint to rule of reason analysis, which requires O'Bannon to allege a "relevant market" and "significant anticompetitive effects."

Under the rule of reason, a restraint is unreasonable if the "restraint's harm to competition outweighs its procompetitive effects." The initial burden is on the plaintiff to show that the restraint produces significant anticompetitive effects within a relevant market.

O'Bannon alleged that the relevant market is the collegiate licensing market, with the products being the rights to use the images of athletes connected with collegiate sports. (Evidence of such a market includes: CLC's representation that it manages "more than 75% share of the college licensing market," and agreements entered into by NCAA and its members, including agreements for the broadcast of athletics events.) The anticompetitive effects are that O'Bannon and those in his class are excluded from competing in that market, which decreases the amount of competitors and reduces the output, such as the amount of available licenses. The allegations were sufficient to overcome a motion for summary judgment.

The court also found that O'Bannon pled sufficient facts to ask for restitution, that is, compensation for a benefit that was obtained unfairly.

The district court looked to different theories that California courts have applied in similar situations. Under one, a court may look to whether a contract was procured by fraud or is otherwise unenforceable; under another, the court may look to see if a defendant obtained a benefit from the plaintiff by fraud or duress; and under yet another, a court may look to see whether a defendant received a benefit and unjustly retained the benefit at the expense of another (unjust enrichment).

Because O'Bannon alleged that CLC profited by brokering licensing agreements for products that contained his image and that the rights to those products were obtained under duress, the court found that his allegations sufficiently supported restitution claims under any of the California theories.

The same day that O'Bannon's case survived dismissal, so did former collegiate football player Samuel Keller's right of publicity suit against the NCAA, CLC, and Electronic Arts.[8] (Keller played quarterback at Arizona State and Nebraska from 2003–2007.) He too called "foul" in their use of his collegiate images. Subsequently, O'Bannon and Keller consolidated their suits into a single complaint (CAC) that included both O'Bannon's antitrust causes of action against the NCAA and CLC and Keller's right of publicity causes of action against NCAA, CLC, and EA. O'Bannon continued as the lead antitrust plaintiff and Keller as the lead right of publicity plaintiff. In addition, O'Bannon added EA as an antitrust defendant as well.

So, the NCAA, CLC, and EA filed motions to dismiss the claims in the CAC. Not surprisingly, the court denied NCAA's and CLC's motions to dismiss the antitrust claims just as it had previously.[9] Judge Wilken did, however, grant EA's motion to dismiss the antitrust claim, stating that O'Bannon had not alleged a sufficient factual basis for either of his antitrust claims against EA.

He had alleged that EA participated in a price-fixing and group boycott/refusal to deal conspiracy, but then said that the

---

8. *See Keller v. Electronic Arts, Inc. et.al.*, 94 USPQ2d 1130, 38 Media L. Rep. 1353, 2010 WL 530108 (N.D. Cal. 2010). Since Keller complained of a violation of his right of publicity against EA (as opposed to the antitrust violation that O'Bannon brought), EA filed a motion to strike that claim pursuant to California's anti-SLAPP statute. The district court denied EA's anti-SLAPP motion to strike. California's anti-SLAPP statute permits a plaintiff to immediately appeal an anti-SLAPP claim to the 9th Circuit, which EA did. EA's appeal triggered the NCAA, CLC, and EA to request a stay of Keller's right of publicity suit and by default O'Bannon's antitrust litigation. On Dec. 17, 2010, the district court stayed all claims as to the right of publicity causes of action, but denied staying the case as to the antitrust claims. *See In re NCAA Student-Athlete Name & Likeness Litigation*, 2101-2 Trade Cases P 77, 273, 2010 WL 5644656 (N.D. Cal. 2010). The right of publicity claims are outside the scope of this chapter.

9. 2011 WL 1642256, United States District Court, N.D. Cal., *In re NCAA Student-Athlete Name & Likeness Licensing Litigation*, No. C 09–1967 CW. May 2, 2011.

agreements that EA entered into with CLC not to compensate O'Bannon were not used in the price-fixing conspiracy. Since he didn't identify any other agreement that linked EA to an alleged price-fixing scheme, the court dismissed those claims. But the court granted O'Bannon leave to amend the CAC to plead with more specificity the antitrust claims against EA. (In the meantime, she required NCAA and CLC to answer the CAC.)

Accordingly, O'Bannon filed a Second Amended Complaint (2CAC) and attempted to explain more specifically how EA was a member of the antitrust conspiracy.[10] O'Bannon alleged that in EA's three licensing agreements with CLC, EA expressly agreed to abide by the NCAA's rules prohibiting student-athlete compensation, and "agreed to extend its agreement with the NCAA, prohibiting compensation to student-athletes, to former student-athletes."

EA filed a motion to dismiss the 2CAC as well. But the court denied EA's motion to dismiss the 2CAC and held that in the 2CAC, O'Bannon pled sufficient facts to sustain an antitrust claim against EA.

As to the price-fixing conspiracy, the court said that O'Bannon added a significant allegation to his complaint: that EA agreed (with CLC and NCAA) not to offer compensation to former student-athletes. He included additional facts, along with the agreements, to show that EA knew that the former student-athletes owned the rights to their images, yet EA intentionally agreed not to compensate them. The additional facts included:

(1) The NCAA's concession at an earlier hearing: "that student-athletes own the rights to their names,

---

10. 2011 WL 2185126 (N.D.Cal.) (Trial Pleading), United States District Court, N.D. Cal., Oakland Division, *In re NCAA Student-Athlete Name & Likeness Licensing Litigation*, No. C 09-01967 CW, May 16, 2011, Second Consolidated Amended Class Action Complaint (2CAC).

images and likenesses at all times but, under NCAA rules, may not exercise them while remaining student-athletes."

(2) Evidence that EA had actually compensated other former student-athletes for using their images on the covers of video games.

Based on these allegations, the court found that ". . . EA was actively participating to ensure that former student-athletes would not receive any compensation for use of their images, likenesses and names," which supported a claim of price-fixing and a group boycott.

EA tried to come from behind again and filed a motion for judgment on the pleadings. However, the court denied that motion for the same reasons it denied EA's motion for summary judgment.

As of the time of publication the case is working its way to trial. O'Bannon hopes to obtain compensation for the former players for the damages they sustained while they were competing and for the "damages sustained by the continued licensing or sale of their images after they ceased participating in collegiate athletics." In addition, he hopes the suit will benefit current students as well by having the "monies generated by the licensing and sale of class members' names, images and likenesses . . . temporarily held in trust . . . until the cessation of their collegiate careers."

To the Hoop 14

First in Class

O'Bannon is trying to certify two classes of athletes under Federal Rule of Civil Procedure 23: (1) former NCAA Division I men's basketball and football players whose images, likenesses and/or names have been included in game footage or in video games since July 21, 2005; and (2) current NCAA Division I men's basketball and football players whose images, likenesses and/or names are included in game footage or in video games during their collegiate careers (although to be compensated afterward).

FRCP 23 sets forth the requirements for bringing and maintaining a class action:

First, under FRCP 23 (a) one or more class members can bring a suit on behalf of the class if:

(1) the class is so numerous that joinder of all members is impracticable;

(2) there are questions of law or fact common to the class;

(3) the claims or defenses of the representative parties are typical of the claims or defenses of the class; and

(4) the representative parties will fairly and adequately protect the interests of the class.

Under FRCP 23 (b), a class may be maintained if prosecuting separate actions certain requirements are met, one of which is:

(3) the court finds that the questions of law or fact common to class members predominate over any questions affecting only individual members, and that a class action is superior to other available methods for fairly and efficiently adjudicating the controversy.

O'Bannon set out to satisfy this "predominance inquiry."

Chapter 15

Movin' the Nets:

Can Private Land Be "Taken" (for the Building of a Sports Arena)?

Goldstein v. Pataki, 488 F. Supp. 2d 254
(E.D.N.Y. 2007), 516 F.3d 50 (2008), *cert denied*,
554 U.S. 930, 128 S. Ct. 2964 (2008); *Goldstein v. UDC*,
64 A.D.3d 168, 879 N.Y.S.2d 524 (N.Y. App. Div. 2009);
Goldstein v. UDC, 13 N.Y.3d 511, 921 N.E.2d 164,
893 N.Y.S.2d 472 (2009)

With Beyonce and JayZ in attendance, the Brooklyn Nets broke ground on their new basketball arena with a well-publicized ceremony on March 11, 2010. But the building of Barclays Center in Brooklyn was riddled with lawsuits and controversy, to say the least.

The biggest issue was whether the State of New York could use its power of eminent domain to force private home and business owners in Brooklyn to sell their land to a private real estate developer, Bruce Ratner, so that he could build a state-of-the-art basketball arena. (Forest City Ratner Company is the company owned by Ratner that carried out the project. Here, "Bruce" or "Ratner" will be used to refer to both the owner and his company.)

You could say it all started in the summer of 2002. After developing the 7-million-square-foot MetroTech Center complex in downtown Brooklyn, Ratner was looking for his next development project. He received a phone call from Brooklyn Borough President Marty Markowitz, who had an idea for another area in Brooklyn, which already had some New York sports history of its own. Marty wanted to revitalize the old rail yard in downtown Brooklyn where Walter O'Malley had sought to build a stadium for the Dodgers in 1957.[1] In 2002, that area, now known as the Atlantic Yards, consisted of two main sections: (1) the Vanderbilt Rail Yard owned by the Metropolitan Transport Authority (MTA), a New York government agency, and (2) a small residential community.

That phone call morphed into a blueprint for a multiuse development with a new (at that point, still New Jersey) Nets basketball arena as its centerpiece. The development would also include a new subway connection, a platform over and reconfiguration of the rail yard, sixteen buildings, which would include residential units, office space, retail space, and community facilities offering health and child care. Ratner teamed up with the New York government agency responsible for economic development, the Empire State Development Corporation (ESDC), to develop the property. Ratner and ESDC jointly announced the project in December 2003.

To actualize the plan, Ratner and ESDC needed to take care of a few "small" preliminary matters:

(1) as the lead agency, ESDC needed to analyze the environmental impact the project would have on the surrounding area and issue an environmental impact statement (EIS);

(2) Ratner needed to acquire the Vanderbilt Rail Yard from the MTA;

---

1. Charles V. Bagli, *A Grand Plan in Brooklyn for the Nets' Arena Complex*, New York Times, Dec. 11, 2003, at B1, 2003 WLNR 5667240. *See also* Charles V. Bagli and Richard Sandomir, *Ratner's Path to Buy Nets had Pitfalls and Promise*, New York Times, Jan. 25, 2004, 2004 WLNR 5414375.

(3) Ratner needed to get the Nets to move from New Jersey to New York;[2] and

(4) Ratner needed to acquire and demolish the properties belonging to private business owners and residents in the Atlantic Yards' footprint.

As to the first matter, on September 15, 2005, ESDC announced that it would conduct public hearings to gauge the public's views on what ESDC should consider in determining the environmental impact the project would have on the area. After those hearings, ESDC issued an environmental impact statement, arguably in compliance with New York's State Environmental Quality Review Act (SEQRA).

Ratner tackled his tasks in tandem with the ESDC. As to item (2), he contacted the MTA to start the process of acquiring the Vanderbilt Yard.[3] For item (3), he purchased the Nets, with the intent to move them to Brooklyn.[4] Finally, for item (4), he purchased several buildings in the project footprint.[5] Each of his tasks brought its own set of controversies and lawsuits. Purchasing the private residences proved to be the toughest.

2. Coincidentally, around this time, YankeeNets owners were looking to split up the ownership of the Yankees, Nets, and Devils. *See* http://www.sportsbusinessdaily. com/Daily/Issues/2003/11/Issue-44/Franchises/Which-Comes-First-A-Yankeenets-Split-Or-A-Nets-Sale.aspx (last visited Sept. 12, 2012). *See also* http://www.nypost. com/p/item_a15TBEuA0aatxb1nfVhjnN (last visited Sept. 12, 2012) and Charles V. Bagli, *YankeeNets Unravels and Teams May Not Move*, New York Times, Aug. 8, 2003, at D1, 2003 WLNR 12729417.

3. Bruce's acquisition of the Vanderbilt Rail Yard spawned its own set of litigation as to the fairness in the bidding process for that land. *See Matter of Montgomery v. MTA*, 2009 N.Y. Slip Op 52539U (New York Co. Sup. Ct. 2009). *See also* Charles V. Bagli and Sewell Chan, *M.T.A. to Deal Only with Ratner on Brooklyn Bid*, New York Times, July 28, 2005, at B1, 2005 WLNR 11822294.

4. There was some controversy there as well. *See* Charles V. Bagli, *Corzine in Bid to Buy Nets and Block Potential Move*, New York Times, Aug. 19, 2003, at D1, 2003 WLNR 5649285.

5. *See Develop Don't Destroy Brooklyn v. Empire State Development Corp.*, 31 AD.3d 144, 148 (May 30, 2006). *See also* New York Times, Dec. 2, 2009, at A30, 2009 WLNR 24290338 and *752 Pacific LLC v. Pacific Carlton Development Corp.*, 14 Misc 3d 1237 (March 1, 2007).

As Ratner was building his Brooklyn empire, those living in and around the Atlantic Yards area began building a counter-effort. Many Brooklyn residents (the Brooklynites) opposed a mammoth development that would change the character of their quaint neighborhood. Most significantly, and the *raison d'être* of this chapter, they did not want Bruce to blow down their homes. Therefore, they founded the community group Develop Don't Destroy Brooklyn (DDDB) to ensure that the Brooklynites' rights and voices were heard amid the building of the project.

Ratner faced staunch resistance (think *Les Miz* without the violence) from residents and business owners who did not want to leave their homes. There were three main holdouts: Daniel Goldstein,[6] Freddy's Bar,[7] and Peter Williams.[8] Goldstein was appointed the name and face of DDDB.[9]

Since Ratner needed all of the land within the Atlantic Yards area to make the project work, acquiring their property was crucial. So, since Ratner had teamed up with ESDC, the state agency responsible for economic development in New

---

6. Daniel Goldstein, along with his wife and daughter, owned a condominium apartment located at 636 Pacific Street since 2003 when the building opened.

7. Freddy's Bar stood at the corner of Dean Street and Sixth Avenue in the Prospect Heights section of Brooklyn for more than seventy years. It has been described as a "neighborhood haven for working-class drinkers, the CBGB's of Brooklyn or a fountainhead of activism, creativity and dissent." *See* Kareem Fahim, *Last Call Looms at Freddy's, in the Path of Atlantic Yards*, New York Times, April 30, 2010, at A18, 2010 WLNR 11822294.

8. Apartment owner Peter Williams brought his own suits in an attempt to keep his home. First, he argued that the eminent domain determination was pursuant to an outdated environmental review and project plan. *See* 2010 WL 3703257 *Peter Williams v. NYSUD & Brooklyn Arena*. Then, he sued to receive compensation for his condemned air rights. *See Peter Williams Enterprises, Inc. v. New York State Urban Development Corp. dba ESDC*, Sept. 20, 2010, unreported 28 Mis 3d 1239 (A), 2010 WL3703264.

9. For an interview with Daniel Goldstein, *see* Brian J. Carreira, The Brooklyn Rail, *A Local Journey: Daniel Goldstein with Brian Carreira*, at http://www.brooklynrail.org/2009/07/local/a-local-journey.

York,[10] he reached out to ESDC to condemn the property on the project's behalf.

Really? Can a private citizen ask a state agency to condemn land for private use?

Yes, but it requires jumping through a few hoops.[11]

First, under N.Y. Eminent Domain Procedure Law (EDPL), ESDC would need to publish a determination stating the public use, benefit, or purpose the condemned land would serve. Then, any condemnee would have thirty days from the determination date to seek a review of this determination. Lastly, the parties would participate in a vesting proceeding to establish the value of the condemned property.

On December 8, 2006, the ESDC issued its determination that it would use its power of eminent domain to condemn Goldstein's (and the other holdouts') property. It determined, after conducting two public hearings and a blight study of the project site, that the condemnation would serve the following public purposes and benefits: eliminate blighted conditions; provide recreational and community facilities; improve the mass transit and infrastructure; provide affordable housing; create jobs; and increase revenues for the city and the state.

The ultimate determination led to numerous lawsuits. This chapter will focus on the federal and state eminent domain lawsuits filed with Goldstein as the named plaintiff. The other plaintiffs consisted of fifteen property owners with homes and businesses in the area slated for condemnation.

---

10. The primary mission of ESDC is to encourage economic investment throughout New York State. It does so in part by promoting large-scale real estate projects that create and retain jobs and or reinvigorate distressed areas. In furtherance of its mission, ESDC has powers to condemn and to override local zoning ordinances. *See DDDB v. ESDC*, 31 AD 3d 144, 146 (May 30, 2006).

11. EDPL § 402 (b)(4). § 201 sets forth the procedures for condemning private property.

On October 27, 2006, Goldstein filed a federal lawsuit in the U.S. District Court for the Eastern District of New York to enjoin the ESDC from taking his home.[12] His primary contention was that the proposed taking of his home violated the Fifth Amendment of the U.S. Constitution, which requires, among other things, that a taking of private property be for public use.

He argued that the ESDC planned to take his property for the sole benefit of Ratner, and that would constitute a private use. Moreover, he argued, even if the taking was ostensibly for public use, it was merely a pretext to benefit Ratner. And, if taken for a pretext, it violates the Fifth Amendment. Finally, he argued that his home was not even blighted: it was just near a blighted area.

The district court said that Goldstein had the public use requirement all wrong. It held that the public use requirement did not necessarily require that condemned land be open to the public for it to use for free. The court explained that condemned land needs to advance a public benefit, which economic development accomplishes.

Accordingly, the court found that the building of a sports arena, the clearing of blight, creation of a new subway entrance, and the building of affordable and new housing qualified as a public benefit.[13] Along those lines, it wasn't up to the judiciary to

---

12. The complaint was initially filed on October 27, 2006, with only the federal claims. It was amended on January 5, 2007, to include state claims pursuant to EDPL § 207, which provides property owners with a thirty-day period in which to seek judicial review once the ESDC declares their property condemned. *See* 2007 WL 575830 (E.D.N.Y.) (Amended Complaint), United States District Court, E.D. N.Y. Jan. 5, 2007.

13. The district court cited the landmark Supreme Court ruling, *Kelo v. City of New London*, 545 U.S. 469,477 (2005). There, the city wanted to revitalize a blighted area by condemning non-blighted property around it as well. In a 5 to 4 decision, the Supreme Court held that: (1) the purpose of economic development satisfies the public use requirement and (2) even if property itself is not blighted, but the area is, then the non-blighted property may be condemned as well.

decide if such economic development was needed; the legislature, the ESDC in this instance, was in a better position to make those local decisions.

Moreover, the court held that even though Goldstein's house in particular wasn't blighted, meaning rundown and slummish, the fact that the area as a whole was blighted was enough to take his house as well.

After finding a valid public use and no evidence to the contrary, the district court held that the taking for the proposed uses was permitted under the U.S. Constitution. Before dismissing Goldstein's case, the court alluded to some occasions when a taking would fail the public use requirement:

(1) if the sole purpose is to transfer property to a private party, or

(2) the purportedly public purpose is really a pretext to bestow a private benefit, which Daniel failed to show.

Nearing homelessness, Goldstein appealed to the U.S. Court of Appeals for the 2d Circuit.

Drawing from the exceptions identified by the district court, Goldstein argued that (1) the taking was unconstitutional because the purpose of the taking was to solely benefit a private party, Ratner, (2) any stated public uses were merely pretexts to benefit Ratner as well, (3) his home was outside the blighted area, and (4) condemned property can't go from private to private citizen—that the government must possess it at some point.

Judge Robert Katzmann, writing for the panel, was sympathetic to Goldstein's plight. He acknowledged that the homeowners wanted to keep their neighborhood, but also said that the law was clear. Even though his heart told him one thing, the law dictated another. (Think ending to *Gone Baby Gone*.)

As to Goldstein's first argument, the court wanted to let Goldstein stay in his home, but like the district court, found that the new arena, new public space, and affordable housing that the condemnation would generate, all served the public purposes of eradicating blight and creating economic development. Considering these factors, the panel had to declare the taking constitutional.

Goldstein supported his second argument by reminding the court that when the project was first announced, Ratner made no mention of eradicating blight. The focus of the announcement was to build excitement for the new Nets arena. It was only after Ratner and ESDC realized they needed to condemn some property that they sought a blight study to comply with the procedures set forth in the EDPL. Goldstein said that this showed the removal of blight was merely a pretext to condemn the area for Ratner's arena. Moreover, Goldstein argued that the government officials who approved the project were improperly motivated by a desire to confer a private benefit on Ratner. He supported this argument by showing the excess in public cost for the project as measured against its benefits.

But the 2d Circuit said none of that matters. Just because a private party benefits does not mean that a condemnation is invalid. Moreover, it would be too intrusive to investigate the officials' motives.

Third, as he did in the court below, Goldstein argued that since his apartment was actually outside of the blighted area, it could not be condemned with the blighted buildings. To that point, Judge Katzmann wrote: "[O]nce shown that the surrounding area is blighted, the state may condemn unblighted parcels as part of an overall plan to improve a blighted area."

Lastly, the court rejected Goldstein's argument that since his property was going straight to a private entity and not a government entity, the taking was amiss. The court held that once it is determined that the project is rationally related to a public use, "it makes no difference that the property will be transferred to private developers, for the power of eminent domain is merely a means to an end."

In affirming the decision of the district court, Judge Katzmann dismissed the federal claims with prejudice and relieved the federal courts in New York of the state claims.

Goldstein was free to file them in state court. And that is what he did. (The threshold issue in Goldstein's state case was whether he missed the statute of limitations for seeking judicial review for the condemnation of his property. Since he amended his federal complaint within the requisite thirty-day period, the New York Supreme Court found he complied with the statute.)

Off to state court he went.

What could Goldstein argue that was different from what he'd already argued at the federal level?

Well, he argued that the state of New York imposes more restrictive standards for the taking of private property than the U.S. Constitution. So, even though the federal court did not find an unconstitutional taking, a court in New York should find that the taking would violate state law.

However, that argument turned out to be just another thrown brick in the project's infrastructure.

Ratner 1, Goldstein 0

First, Goldstein argued that the taking would violate the Public Use Clause of the New York Constitution because "public use" under New York law means that the property must be held open for use by all members of the public for free.

The court found, however, that New York jurisprudence advises against such a literal reading—that public use refers to uses that inure a benefit onto the public. For example, back in the day, a railroad was considered a public use even though one couldn't get a free ride. Similarly, the court found that safe-guarding the public from the menace caused by blighted or slum conditions confers a public benefit. In addition, unlike the Fifth Amendment, section 207 of the EDPL expressly states that a taking may be for a "public use, benefit or purpose."[14]

Ratner 2, Goldstein 0

Okay, so even if a taking for a public use, benefit, or purpose is acceptable, Goldstein contended that the taking wouldn't serve any of those purposes.

The court disagreed with Goldstein yet again. It held that where land has been found to be substandard, its taking for urban renewal constitutes a public purpose. Likewise, here, the public benefit is the clearing of slums, the creation of an arena, publicly accessible open space, affordable housing, improvements to public transit, and new job opportunities.

Ratner 3, Goldstein 0

Goldstein further contended that even if there is a public benefit, it is incidental to the private benefit that will be realized by Bruce Ratner.

But the court said that, since so much of the land acquired is substandard, and the taking is rationally related to the purpose of remedying these substandard conditions, any incidental profit that may inure to Ratner doesn't undercut the public purpose: "[W]here the public good is expected to be enhanced by a project, it does not matter that private interests might be benefited."

Ratner 4, Goldstein 0

Goldstein also argued that the project contravenes another section of the New York Constitution on how state funds may be spent.

---

14. *Goldstein v. UDC*, 64 A.D.3d 168, 879 N.Y.S.2d 524 (N.Y. A.D., 2009)..

He asserted that Section 6 of Article XVIII of the New York Constitution dictates that any state funds that are used to defray infrastructure costs of new construction must solely go toward new housing units for low-income persons.

The court disagreed again. The court said that the article was created to serve two purposes: (1) provide low-income housing and (2) clear and rehabilitate a substandard area. Basically, the earmark requirement only applies where the building of low-income housing is the sole purpose of the project. The housing restriction does not apply in this situation, that is, where the purposes of the project are to both provide low-income housing and rehabilitate substandard land through improvements.

Ratner 5, Goldstein 0

Lastly, Goldstein argued that the proposed condemnation violated his due process and equal protection rights under the New York Constitution. The court also rejected this argument, finding instead that ESDC had substantially complied with the procedural requirements of the EDPL by conducting two community forums and public hearings. Meeting those procedural requirements was equivalent to meeting the due process requirement under the New York Constitution. In addition, the court found no evidence to support Goldstein's contention that he was treated differently from others similarly situated in violation of the equal protection clause.

Therefore, on May 12, 2009, the Appellate Division, Second Department, denied his challenge to the condemnation of his home.

As a side note, you might be wondering (as was the ESDC), why the state court didn't just dismiss the claims under the doctrine of collateral estoppel, where once the same issue is litigated and determined in a prior action, one is proscribed from litigating that same issue again. The court said it was not the same issue. The question in the 2d Circuit was whether the proposed taking violated the Fifth Amendment of the U.S. Constitution. In state court, the question was whether the taking violated the procedure set forth in the EDPL. Although they turned out to be similar arguments, the issues were not identical.

The New York Court of Appeals sealed Goldstein's fate. Well, his condo's fate.[15]

It agreed with the lower court's finding that New York recognizes the act of rehabilitating a blighted area as a public use under the New York Constitution. The Court of Appeals determined that the blight need not meet those of the "great depression," but substandard and unsanitary conditions suffice. Moreover, the legislature can make such fact-dependent determinations as to blight and the need for economic development.

Although Goldstein had a supporter in the dissent, the majority held that the ESDC had the power to condemn Goldstein's property. So, on November 24, 2009, the New York Court of Appeals rejected Goldstein's challenge to the taking of his home via eminent domain and dismissed the case, paving the way for the construction of Barclays Center.

By the end of the year, Ratner had state bonds issued to complete the financing of the Atlantic Yards project.[16] The following March, title transferred from the property owners to the

---

15. *Matter of Goldstein v New York State Urban Dev. Corp.*, 13 N.Y.3d 511, 921 N.E.2d 164, 893 N.Y.S.2d 472, 2009 N.Y. Slip Op. 08677, Court of Appeals of New York, argued Oct. 14, 2009, decided Nov. 24, 2009. Motion to Reargue was denied by the Court of Appeals on Feb. 18, 2010.

16. John Brennan, *Nets Bond Sale Generates $511M, Deal Big Part of Brooklyn Arena's Financing*, New Jersey Record, Dec. 16, 2009, at A05, 2009 WLNR 26391669.

ESDC, en route to Ratner.[17] Goldstein ended up receiving $3 million for the rights to his condo.[18]

On April 30, 2012, the Nets announced a new logo, uniform, and name—the Brooklyn Nets. Partial Nets owner JayZ performed the first concert at Barclays Center on Sept. 28, 2012.

---

17. *In the Matter of the Application of the New York State Urban Development Corporation d/b/a Empire State Development.* 26 Misc.3d 1228(A), Supreme Court, Kings County, New York. Corporation to acquire title in fee simple absolute to certain real property and a temporary easement in certain real property, required for the Atlantic Yards Land Use Improvement and Civic Project—Phase 1., No. 32741/09. March 1, 2010.

18. *See* http://observer.com/2011/10/is-dan-goldstein-really-as-bad-as-bruce-ratner-just-because-he-wants-a-renovation/.

To the Hoop 15

That Was Not the End of the Battle for Atlantic Yards

The project is still entrenched in other pending lawsuits from diehard Brooklynites, with claims ranging from violations of environmental law[1] to infringement of air rights.[2] Moreover, reports began to show unkept promises. In March 2011, the *New York Times* reported that the buildings would be using modular construction, which residents argued was inferior to other building materials.[3] As of May 29, 2012, the building of the promised 400 low- and middle-income housing units was pushed back, potentially years,[4] and as of June 7, 2012, construction of the Long Island Railroad train yard was delayed.[5] Further, there were reports that Ratner was in need of money.[6] He had already sold 80 percent of the Nets and 45 percent of the arena to Russian billionaire Mikhail Prokhorov while the eminent domain cases were pending.

Overall, the Atlantic Yards project accomplished "what the developer dreamed and Brooklynites dreaded:" it revitalized the area with new businesses, storefronts, and higher rents.[7]

The bottom line is: federal courts have equated public purpose with public use under the Takings Clause of the Fifth Amendment. In New York, specifically, the elimination of blight for the building of a basketball arena has been deemed a public purpose.

---

1. *See DDDB v. ESDC (DDDB II)*, Supreme Court, New York County, New York. July 13, 2011, 33 Misc.3d 330927 N.Y.S.2d 571 *affd*, *DDDB v. ESDC*, Supreme Court, Appellate Division, First Department, New York. April 12, 2012. 94 A.D.3d 508, 942 N.Y.S.2d 477, and related cases.

2. *See Peter Williams Enters., Inc. v New York State Urban Dev. Corp.* 2010 WL 3703257.

3. *See* Charles V. Bagli, *A Federal Case and Modular Building Plan Bring New Attention to Atlantic Yards Project*, New York Times, March 18, 2011, at A25, 2011 WLNR 5342322.

4. Eliot Brown, *Housing Pieces Delayed*, Wall St. J. Abstracts (USA), May 29, 2012, at A15, 2012 WLNR 11310072.

5. Eliot Brown and Ted Mann, *LIRR Faces New Delay: Brooklyn Train Yard*, Wall St. J. Abstracts (USA), June 7, 2012, at A21, 2012 WLNR 11974196.

6. *See* Charles V. Bagli, *Russian Billionaire Steps Closer to Buying the Nets*, New York Times, Dec. 17, 2009, at B18, 2009 WLNR 25369117.

7. http://www.nytimes.com/2012/04/17/nyregion/atlantic-yards-project-is-already-transforming-brooklyn.html?pagewanted=all (visited June 23, 2012).

Chapter 16

Double-Double:
Was the NCAA's Final Four Ticket Drawing an Illegal Lottery?

George v. Nat'l Collegiate Athletic Ass'n,
2009 WL 6965794, not reported in F. Supp. 2d
(S.D. Ind. 2009), *rev'd,* 613 F.3d 658 (7th Cir. 2010),
vacated, 623 F.3d 1135 (7th Cir. 2010), *answering
certified question,* 945 N.E.2d 150 (Ind. 2011),
439 F. App'x 544 (7th Cir. 2011)

Tom George[1] applied for tickets to the 2009 NCAA Men's Basketball Championship Game between Michigan State and the University of North Carolina. He submitted an entry form and payment for the face value of ten tickets, as well as a $6 service fee for each ticket. Because more people requested tickets than there were seats in the arena, the NCAA conducted a random drawing to determine which applicants would receive their requested tickets. George was on the losing end. The NCAA reimbursed him for the face value of the tickets, but not for the service fee. So he was out $60, just for applying.

Upon losing his bid for championship tickets, George brought a class action suit against the NCAA and Ticketmaster

---

1. It is not clear whether George actually applied for the maximum amount of tickets. Since he was the named plaintiff in the class action, I am using his name for what the complaint alleges.

in federal court, claiming they ran an illegal lottery in their allocation of the tickets. An illegal lottery consists of consideration (something of value, usually money that is exchanged) for a chance (usually indicated by a random drawing as opposed to a game of skill) to win a prize. George argued that the per-ticket service fee he paid and lost constituted consideration for the chance to win the prize—NCAA Men's Basketball Championship tickets.

On first look, the U.S. District Court for the Southern District of Indiana dismissed his case based on the equitable doctrine of *in pari delicto*, which means "where the wrong of both parties is equal, the position of the defendant is the stronger."

In other words, the court dismissed the case because it determined that George knew the transaction was wrong, but participated nonetheless. Accordingly, the district court found that even if the NCAA's ticket distribution practices constituted an illegal lottery, George was aware of how the system worked when he applied for tickets and couldn't cry foul after the fact.

On appeal, the U.S. Court of Appeals for the 7th Circuit initially agreed with George. Applying the definition of a lottery in Indiana to the facts of the NCAA ticket allocation system, it found consideration, chance, and a prize in the (1) per-ticket or per-entry fee, (2) the random drawing, and (3) the scarce and valuable tickets. Thus, the 7th Circuit held that the NCAA's system fell into the framework of an illegal lottery.

In addition, the 7th Circuit found that the legal doctrine relied on by the district court, *in pari delicto*, didn't apply. The court stated that *in pari delicto* only applies when there is a mutual agreement between the parties to engage in an illegal lottery. In this case, there was nothing to indicate that George was in cahoots with the NCAA to break the law or that he knew he was participating in an illegal lottery when he attempted to purchase tickets.

Although it appeared the NCAA ticket allocation system was illegal, that turned out not to be the case.

The NCAA asked the court to reconsider its opinion. The 7th Circuit agreed to rehear the case. But, before taking it up again, it asked the Indiana Supreme Court to weigh in on Indiana law.

The 7th Circuit certified three questions to the Indiana Supreme Court:

(1) Do the plaintiffs' allegations about the NCAA's method for allocating scarce tickets to championship tournaments describe a lottery that would be unlawful under Indiana law?

(2) If the plaintiffs' allegations describe an unlawful lottery, would the NCAA's method for allocating tickets fall within the Ind. Code § 35–45–5–1(d) exception for "bona fide business transactions that are valid under the law of contracts"?

(3) If the plaintiffs' allegations describe an unlawful lottery, do the plaintiffs' allegations show that their claims are subject to an *in pari delicto* defense?

The Indiana Supreme Court set out to answer the first question first (seems like a good tactic). In doing so, it examined Indiana's statute on lotteries. It determined that the term "lottery" means a scheme for the distribution of prizes by lot or chance among those who provided or promised to provide consideration. Under this definition, the court noted the necessary three essential elements to a lottery: (1) a prize, (2) chance, and (3) consideration.

Unlike the 7th Circuit, the Indiana Supreme Court found that the NCAA's system lacked a prize.

To the Hoop 16

Bottom Line

Keep in mind, this decision only validates the NCAA's ticket allocation system under Indiana law. Each state may have its own definition of prizes. According to a press release from the law firm representing George and the class that sued NCAA, Ticketmaster refunded the application fees paid by those customers who didn't win tickets to the NCAA 2009 Men's Basketball Championship. The press release also indicated that the NCAA appeared to have changed its ticketing policies in that it no longer allows multiple entries for ticketing lotteries and, if a fan doesn't win tickets, the application fee is returned in full.

Well, then, what would you call the tickets to the NCAA Men's Basketball Championship?

The Indiana Supreme Court said that a prize is something worth more than the market value, and because the NCAA distributed tickets at the market value, by definition, the tickets could not be a prize.

Okay, but who determines the market value?

George argued that the fact that one can sell tickets for more than he or she paid indicates that the market value is higher than the value paid.

The Indiana Supreme Court basically said that the event itself determines the market value, since there is no market for tickets until the event issues the tickets in the first place. So, as a matter of law, the face value of the tickets equals the market value of the tickets.

It explained that where the applicants do not "venture small sums for the chance of obtaining a larger value," and instead invest the actual price of the tickets in exchange for either the tickets or the entire amount invested, the price paid equals the market value. Consequently, when you pay the market value, what you receive is not a prize.

To exemplify this point, the Indiana Supreme Court described a situation where one pays $20 for a coin worth $100,000. In that case, the value of the coin is set by a different party. The issuer did not create the fair market value of the coin. With Final Four tickets the NCAA creates the primary market for event tickets. The fair-market value of the tickets, then, is the face value as set by the NCAA. There is no secondary market at the time the tickets are issued.

Based on its definition of "prize," the Indiana Supreme Court concluded that as there was no "prize," there was no "lottery," because at the time applicants submitted to the NCAA their offers to purchase tickets, the market value equaled the face value of the tickets. Thus, as a matter of law, the NCAA's ticket-distribution plan is not a lottery.

Okay, so Indiana reasons that if what you get is worth no more than what you put in, it is not a prize. But what about the service fee—isn't that consideration since you lose it if you don't receive the tickets?

The Indiana Supreme Court continued to explain that since the prize factor was absent, it did not need to look to the consideration analysis since all three factors are needed for an illegal lottery.

Thus, the Indiana Supreme Court determined that the NCAA's ticket-distribution process was not an illegal lottery under Indiana law and, therefore, declined to reach the remaining questions presented. After receiving its answer from the Indiana Supreme Court, the 7th Circuit issued a new decision, affirming the district court and finding that the NCAA did not conduct an illegal lottery in its prize allocation system.

Index

About the Author

Melissa Altman Linsky is an Adjunct Professor of Sports Law at Emory University School of Law in Atlanta, Georgia.

She received her bachelor's degree in communication from UCLA and her law degree from Emory. After graduating law school, she practiced trademark law at Knobbe, Martens, Olson & Bear, LLP, in Orange County, California. Upon moving back to Atlanta, she took a temporary position in the trademark group at Turner Broadcasting Systems, Inc., and when Turner sold the Atlanta Hawks, the Atlanta Thrashers, and operating rights to Philips Arena to Atlanta Spirit, LLC, she ultimately joined the new company and assisted with setting up its legal department. At Atlanta Spirit, Melissa provided legal counsel to all departments within the sports and entertainment enterprise: from the telemarketers to the ticket promoters, from the sponsorship sellers to the game operators, from the talent bookers to the arena staffers, from the basketball and hockey managers to the chief officers. She also worked with counsel from the NBA and NHL to ensure compliance with their respective rules, regulations, guidelines and collective bargaining agreements. In addition to teaching, Melissa consults on sports and marketing legal issues.